LIVE *Your* DREAM

second edition

Discover and Achieve
Your Life Purpose

By

Joyce Chapman, M.A.

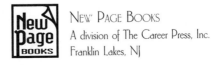
NEW PAGE BOOKS
A division of The Career Press, Inc.
Franklin Lakes, NJ

LIVE YOUR DREAM 2ND EDITION
Typeset By Eileen Dow Munson
Cover design by Cheryl Cohan Finbow
Printed in the U.S.A. by Book-mart Press

To order this title, please call toll-free 1-800-CAREER-1 (NJ and Canada: 201-848-0310) to order using VISA or MasterCard, or for further information on books from Career Press.

The Career Press, Inc., 3 Tice Road, PO Box 687
Franklin Lakes, NJ 07417
www.careerpress.com
www.newpagebooks.com

Library of Congress Cataloging-in-Publication Data

Chapman, Joyce.
    Live your dream : discover and achieve your life purpose / by Joyce Chapman.— 2nd ed.
        p. cm.
    Includes index.
    ISBN 1-56414-532-8 (pbk.)
    1. Self-actualization (Psychology) I. Title.

BF637.S4 C459 2002
158.1—dc21

                                                                    2001031242

Acknowledgments

I want to thank all the wonderful authors and teachers whose ideas have helped me to learn and grow. I invite all those who benefit from reading this book to share their experiences with me by writing and helping to advance this work. Thank you also to all the "Live Your Dream" workshop participants and clients who with open hearts shared their own growth to enrich this book. Thanks especially to my family for their unfailing encouragement and for helping to make it possible for me to live my dream of creating this book.

I also want to thank Eva Ditler and Nancy Reid-Edwards for the time, efforts, and amazing talents that they expended as members of my dream team. With their support I have been empowered to live my dream of the revision of this book.

My special appreciation goes to Diane Chalfant, whose knowledge and expertise in the fields of human potential work, New Thought, psychology, writing, and editing have molded my ideas and years of experience into the form of the first edition of this book.

Names and other identifying features have been altered to respect the confidentiality of shared life stories. Some of the character examples and situations represent composites drawn from several individuals who experienced and shared similar stories.

Welcome to the realization of your dream!

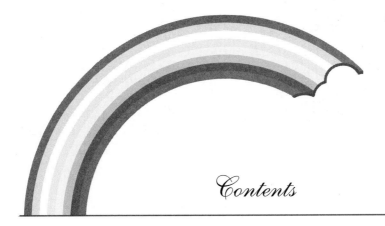

Contents

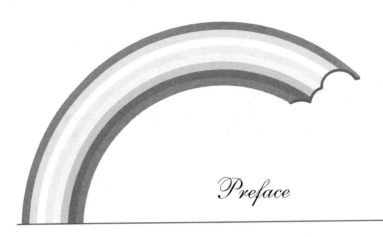

Preface

*A*re you *living your dream?* What would your life be like if you were doing the exact thing that would make you completely happy? What if you spent most of your time doing what you enjoy and love doing the most? What skills would you develop to fully express your natural creative ability? What parts of your life might be left behind if you moved into a fuller expression of your true potential? What, exactly, *is* your dream? What would it look like? How would you feel, look, and act?

Are you living five out of seven days of each week of your life waiting to say, "Thank God it's Friday!" Are you putting up with less than you deserve? Do you feel you deserve less than complete happiness and self-fulfillment? Have you put a dream on hold? Have you given up your dream? Do you remember having one? Is your dream an "impossible dream"? How do you reconcile your dream with what our life is like right now?

Where do we learn to live our dream? Who teaches that class? What are the requirements? How do you discover what your own unique dream really is? What steps must be taken to get there from where you are now?

This book has been created to guide you in answering these questions. You will discover that you have the answers within your grasp. As you read the exercises and examples you will likely begin your journey toward realizing your dream.

You will be invited to take a close look at yourself. You can explore what it is you really want, what is important to you, and write your answers in your Dream Journal and *The Live Your Dream Workbook* to bring the learning into your life. You can design a map and a create a guide for yourself as you begin living your dream, as well as gain tools and techniques for realizing it.

Since the first edition of *Live Your Dream,* I have been privileged to receive many calls, letters, and e-mails from readers who have asked questions to gain clarification or inspiration. Some of the questions, and answers, are included in the first six chapters of this revised second edition.

As you live your dream, your radiance will energize everything around you. Your shift in consciousness will empower both yourself and others. Your dream path will feel natural and right for you, and your experience of love and joy will expand exponentially.

What if you really did everything it takes? Could you actually dare to live true to yourself and achieve all your dreams? Could you have what you say you want? Is it scary? Are you willing to give it a try? Then let's begin!

—Joyce Chapman

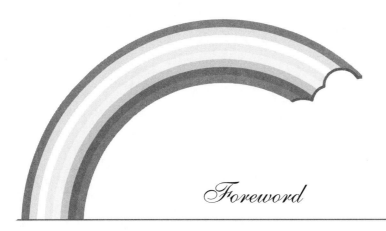

Foreword

*I*t's easy to get lost these days in the complex jungle of modern life, to become confused, to not know where you're going or even if you're going in the right direction. Are you doing what you really want to do, or doing what you've been told to do, or doing what you think you should do?

Live Your Dream is a book that assists you in defining your life, your vision, and your goals. It teaches what you need to do to make your hidden aims possible and how to actually make your secret dreams come true.

Through this thorough, step-by-step process you are shown how to remove obstacles, conflicts, and resistance. To establish new values, habits, abilities, and possibilities. To get the results, support, and satisfaction you have always craved. To let go of being a powerless victim of the past and become a powerful successful victor in the present.

This book was lovingly and compassionately put together by a master teacher who has created a comprehensive learning system that covers all the bases and leaves nothing to chance. It will require effort, commitment, and discipline, but if you practice her directions, results are sure to follow.

Joseph Campbell said, "Follow your bliss." In this book, Joyce Chapman shows you how.

—Bernard Gunther, Ph.D.
Author, *Sense Relaxation and Energy Ecstasy*

CHAPTER ONE

Defining the Dream

*You are never given a wish without also
being given the power to make it true.
You may have to work for it, however.*

—Richard Bach, *Illusions*

*H*ow will you express who you are, in this lifetime? What is the greatest achievement you can imagine yourself accomplishing? What is the greatest contribution you could possibly make? What is the mark you would make on the world if you were in charge of your life—if there were no reasons or excuses why not? What is the greatest *you* can imagine being? The purpose of this book is to assist you in actively being the person you want to be and in acquiring the tools and mastering the skills to achieve your ultimate potential.

If someone walked up to you and told you, "You can have your life only if you take a step toward living your dream *today,*" how would you respond? Well, life *is* saying just that—each and every moment—to you. If you're not busy living to your fullest potential, parts of you are busy fading away.

In his famous "I Have a Dream" speech in 1963, Martin Luther King, Jr. moved an entire nation to aspire to his vision of freedom and equality for all. Albert Schweitzer and Mother Teresa have inspired the world with their selfless commitment to care for the poor and the sick. Throughout history, great artists, musicians, poets, scientists, inventors, writers, thinkers, and leaders have left us the legacy of their dreams for making the world a better place in which to live. Enough dreams remain for you to assume your rightful place among the dreamers—and doers—of the world.

Here are some of the comments made by people in my "Live Your Dream" workshops as they began to explore the implications of living their dreams.

I don't know what my dream is. I'd love to discover it. That would be juicy for me!

With a husband and three small children, house, Little League, ballet lessons, PTA, and all the rest, putting myself last just became so easy and natural—last on the long list of things to do that I never got to the bottom of. I need to get back in touch with *my* feelings, *my* dreams. I want to have time to work on me, so what I give back to my family is *quality*—the best I can be.

I want the magical to be real. I want more than I feel is actually possible in real life. You see I live this responsible, organized, but all too boring existence, with one eye always on the lookout for Prince Charming to come along and sweep me off my feet. So I'm naturally attracted to people with the thrill of great, momentous drama going on in their lives. It's as if I want to adopt their drama in place of my own missing one—a real, rich, fully lived life of my own.

I thought I could find more fulfillment if I gave up teaching and went into business for myself. I thought if I made it to the top of my field, developing a successful practice and becoming a prestigious executive, that would satisfy me. Having accomplished this, I realize that through it all, I've been aware of this little nagging doubt telling me, "There has to be *more*." Now I'm at an age where I thought I would just curl up on the sofa, take life easy, and enjoy it all. But how dull! My life is not over yet. I've just discovered I have a *bigger* dream than ever, now. I'm planning to open my own school for entrepreneurs.

It seemed as if there was really nothing I wanted. My house is just the way I like it. My marriage may not be pure enchantment, but it's pretty good. My career is satisfactory—or so I thought. Then I realized, as long as I pretended everything was okay, I would never have to stretch. I keep lots of "saviors" in my life— comfortable people who shield me from having to stretch. But when I finally stopped to listen to the stillness of what my life has settled into, I heard a much lower roar than what I'd like.

Don't talk to me about being happy and prosperous. I have all I can do just to pay my bills.

"I'm so busy living your nightmare, I have no room for any dream of my own!" The moment I heard myself say this to my husband, I knew I must take the "Live Your Dream" workshop. But what an incongruent time! My marriage was breaking up; I was being wrenched apart by conflict and fear, and the desolation of loss seemed all the future had to hold for me. Yet those words jarred me into realizing that for 16 years of our marriage, my dreams were not *my* dreams, but *his* dreams. I raced around frantically supporting my husband in every rash decision he seemed compelled to make, picking up all the loose ends, trying to make it work somehow, providing the backup to make *his* every wish possible. I finally saw that it was my dream, from now on, that would give me the vision to move forward and make a life for myself. I must move beyond the nightmare and into the dream.

If you don't have a dream, your life will be about your problems. The matters of "greatest consequence," claiming your attention during most of your waking hours, will revolve around what to worry about next. You can exist and subsist, and you may be tempted to deceive yourself into believing that that's enough to satisfy you. Have a party; play a game; play dress-up; the television is always there to hand out a vicarious existence—more glamorous and exciting than the lonely living room or the battling kids. But in the space where the burning desire and the passion for living belong, there is a black hole of desolation, drawing you down into oblivion. Your life force is draining away, as your energy and your aliveness and your vitality discover no other viable outlet for expression.

Once you have defined your dream, everything else in your life becomes just things to handle. The overflowing sink, the spilled milk, and the rush to get off to work in the morning all assume a different perspective in the light of your dream. They become mere situations to take care of so you can get on with the more important work of your dream. They are no longer matters of utmost significance—your dream is!

People who are following their dreams live their everyday lives differently. They walk differently. They buy flowers differently—with the intent to be their best. When your life is about your dream, you are always living true to yourself and your dreams. You're constantly striving to go further, to make the most of the present moment. Each problem becomes just a challenge to be overcome, an opportunity made for learning. You will do whatever it takes to get to where you need to be.

When I was a child, I dreamed of being a teacher. I would teach the world from the top of the doghouse in my backyard. At seven, I taught my 5-year-old neighbor to read. And I did, in fact, go on to enjoy a successful teaching career for 20 years. I loved finding a way to draw out that creative spark from within each individual.

Once that dream had been fully expressed, I found myself asking, "What's the *greatest* teaching I have to offer?" A new, bigger dream began to take form. I began to ask, "What would be necessary to assist people in completely fulfilling themselves?" At first I didn't realize that the "people" I was talking about was really myself.

I began teaching a journaling workshop, guiding people to listen to their inner truth and know themselves from the inside out. Soon a further need became apparent: What comes next? How do you move from self-knowing to expressing yourself in the world? How do you move beyond all the barriers and learn to be the person you want to be? I didn't have a manual for that. Thus, "Live Your Dream" was born.

Then one day I noticed a billboard that said, "To Be Rich & Famous." *That's it!* I thought. *To be rich and famous, by being exactly who I am!* "But that's silly and egotistical," my rational mind said, as it set to work to cancel the idea. However, I had learned by now to honor the messages that come from within.

Gradually, the dream of teaching others how to be exactly who they are unfolded. Let the farmers be great farmers. Let the artists create great art. Let the builders construct masterful cathedrals. Let the parents create wonderful children and the singers sing beautiful songs, with all individuals following their own inner guidance and expressing their unique talents in the way they love most, all free to live their own truth. People who are expressing themselves creatively have no need to fight. My dream was about bringing peace on Earth.

The dream took on gigantic proportions. To follow it, I decided to go back to school, at the age of 51, for more information and a master's degree in counseling psychology. Balancing career, family, school ("Can I really go back to school *now?*"), and a dream—could I do it? It was no longer a choice for me. Accomplishing and living my dream was my *life*.

Everywhere I offered my "Live Your Dream" workshops, people were hungry for more. They responded as if they had just been awakened from a heavy sleep, to see before them all their brightest dreams as a reality. They leapt at the invitation to simply "live true to who you are." As they completed the homework, they began to come back to *life—their* life.

As this work continues, my life has expanded beyond my wildest imagination. I've reached heights I never considered possible. I feel more alive than I ever have before. Living true to my dream touches every aspect of my life. My husband and children have encouraged me and have supported this work by sharing their own experiences of the "Live Your Dream" principles with me. My work vitalizes and revitalizes me.

Your dream can do the same for you. But its possibilities should come with a prominent warning: This work could be hazardous to your status quo. The changes you make may be difficult, even painful, at times. You may have to let go of things you've been clinging to or are comfortable with to make room for your new, expanded experience. In the process, you will find where your passion lies. You will discover the source of your enthusiasm, and as you do the exercises and begin to express aspects of yourself more fully, you will experience a growing sense of inner peace and fulfillment and a tremendous aliveness and connectedness with *life!* You will become the *actualized dreamer.*

Discovering and identifying their dreams seem to be challenges for many people. We are often trained to live according to someone else's idea of what we *should* be or do. The inner knowing we once possessed lies buried beneath years and years of second-best living. And we are taught to be modest, to be content with what we have and not ask for or expect more. We suppress our own wishes and desires and deny ourselves the very experiences that bring us to life. The truth we live is someone else's rather than our own.

Here are some dreams that my clients have shared with me:

I wanted to be the greatest gymnast in the world—but my parents never took me seriously. And I guess I don't take myself seriously, even now. I'm just an average person. I think my biggest dream these days is to get a good night's sleep.

My dream was to raise two wonderful kids. Now that that's done, I have nowhere else to go. What's going to be my reason for getting up in the morning and feeling good? I have to have a dream.

Denise had been an editor for seven years. Her intermittent, heavy sighs punctuated the air with her despair and disinterest in her job. In every free minute, she could be overheard on the phone, cheering up the sick and troubled members of her church. "What would I ever tell my dad, if I wanted to leave a respected position like this, and go become 'just' a secretary for the church?" she agonized.

Austin has established a successful medical practice, but over the years his work has come to hold less and less appeal for him. "Whose dream was it that I should become a doctor?" he begins to ponder. "Surely not *mine*! I think I'd be happiest making beautiful furniture in my own woodworking shop."

Other people have no trouble conceiving their dreams, but whether through fear, lack of perseverance, disbelief in themselves, or an unwillingness to take the risk, the original conception is as far as they go. Here are some other dreams people have shared with me:

When I was young, I used to dream of changing the world. In middle age, I've had to realize that maybe the biggest impact I'll ever have is just the little things I do for the few people close to me. The world has passed me by now. I'm too old for dreams.

My dreams? So many have come and gone. But they never seem to get beyond the "terrific idea" stage. Maybe I give up too easily or I don't try hard enough. There's definitely a gap, for me, between dreaming the dream and actually *living* it—knowing how to get from here to there.

My dream is to make *millions* as a trial lawyer. But the truth is, I wear a uniform that says I'm a bell captain.

✧◆✧

Still others have doggedly pursued yesterday's dream, neglecting to see that it has died and should have been peacefully buried long ago.

I don't like what I do, but it's the only thing I know.

Only 15 years to go 'till retirement. I'll just bide my time and build up the benefits. I'd lose too much if I considered changing jobs now.

I still keep hoping someday my husband will change and become the person who can make me happy.

✧◆✧

If you're still hanging on to a dead dream of yesterday, laying flowers on its grave by the hour, you cannot be planting the seeds for a new dream to grow today. So take a look at whatever blocks you from doing what you really want to do. Write them down, and study each one. Is it worth selling your soul for? Really consider what's at stake. It's your life, and you choose it, minute to minute to minute.

Unlike goals, which are set in place fairly logically, your dream can only come from deep within. When I was teaching small children, I would make a point of asking, "What do you think is the best way for you to learn this?" The child would *always* tell me. Inside themselves, all children naturally have direction. We are not born without direction. All we have to do is bring it forth. You can let that direction and that dream surface, take shape and attain clarity in your mind's eye. The exercises in this chapter are designed to trigger associations and guide you to your inner knowing of exactly what your dream is.

Your dream may peek shyly through a crack in your awareness at first, or it may present itself boldly and dramatically. Your challenge will be to pay attention to the messages you receive from your inner guidance.

Kathy, who attended one of my first "Live Your Dream" workshops, shared:

> "There's a tiny thought inside me—you'd probably laugh—I see myself on the cover of *Vogue* magazine!" When she explored the idea further, she came to this realization: "The times I feel really *alive* are when I'm right down in the arena. I thrive on being a participant. It pushes me to be my best, in a way that sitting up in the stands as a spectator can never do."

Today Kathy is a successful model, traveling in Europe and calling her time her own—also part of her dream. She's enjoying her life tremendously and living so prosperously that she simply smiled contentedly when her mother asked her, "When are you going to settle down and get a *real* job?" Kathy can understand her mother's point of view and appreciates her concern. But she knows that her dream job *is* her real job. Her vision has made it possible for her to make a dream life a reality. She doesn't have to settle for a nine-to-five job and somebody else's problems. And she would never have gotten there without stopping to honor that "tiny thought" that bubbled up from her subconscious mind.

"Don't be ridiculous!" Debra's rational mind said, when she realized her secret desire was to be a minister. "You have all these *responsibilities*. With your husband changing jobs and the kids needing so much attention and chauffeuring…and you'd have to go back to school. It's just not *practical*!" Yet as Debra looked more closely at her life, she declared in anguish, "If I don't have a dream soon, I'm going to be swallowed up by the turmoil all around me." She was so used to living at the effect of everything in her life, that to think of being the *cause* introduced whole new possibilities.

What she wanted more than anything else was to live as the spiritual self she was beginning to uncover, where she found peace and inner assurance. And what better way than to teach what she loved, which was the Scriptures? She also realized that the times she felt absolutely her best were when she got all dressed up and went into what she called her "presentation mode."

"Where there's a will, there's got to be a way," Debra resolved, as she soon found herself handling what had been a full-time load in half the time, with surprisingly ample energy left over for her classes.

Imagine that you can take a picture of your life, focusing your imaginary camera clearly on its central subject: your dream. Then all the other parts of the "picture" will come into focus as well.

You may have many dreams, or you may be unsure whether the dream you identify now is your ultimate dream. My experience has shown that living your dream is a cyclical process; no sooner has one dream bowed offstage than the next is waiting in the wings. Working through each successive dream to its completion is a powerful means of honing in on your most magnificent self.

It often happens that through the act of identifying a dream and beginning to build it, people learn something unexpected about themselves. In one of my workshops, a shy woman mentioned that she had always wanted to sing publicly. She was given an assignment: to go sing in a piano lounge where members of the audience were invited to come up on stage and perform. She came away from this experience with a positive certainty: "That is *not* what I want to do." It took declaring her intention and then following it up with decisive action to gain this knowledge. Without these steps, she could easily have spent the rest of her life tentatively humoring the possibility—and feeling inadequate and ineffective about carrying it through. The experience brought her instant clarity. Her attention was freed to move on and discover what she really *did* want to do.

Your dream can be as simple or complex as you desire. And like mine, your dream may unfold to greater and greater dimensions as you become committed to it. No matter what your dream is, the important point is that you declare one and dedicate yourself to it.

Your dream is as close as your own mental image of it. How many of us go through our lives troubled by a vague sense that the person we *are* is not the person we really *want* to be? But we don't stop to define precisely who that desired person would be. We know what we don't want, but exactly what *do* we want and need? We can easily picture what makes us unhappy, but we don't give much thought to what makes us happy!

If you can close your eyes and picture your dream, you can bring it forth in your experience. Your subconscious mind, that part of you that goes to work creating whatever reality you choose to believe in, is the source of what becomes real in your outer experience. You can learn to direct your conscious mind to plant ideas in your subconscious mind that will manifest happiness rather than unhappiness. You can put your subconscious mind to work in the service of your highest thoughts and dreams. Otherwise, it will continue proving the validity of pessimism and complacency.

The exercises here will help you picture the many facets of your dream clearly and in detail. You can go on from there to plant the beliefs in your subconscious mind that will flower into the realization of your dream. Subsequent exercises will guide you, step by step, to take the actions necessary to bring your dream into being.

As you work through these exercises, it is important to follow some basic guidelines:

✦ Be gentle with yourself and others. The place where you are right now is perfect for you! Look how far you've come—and how well you have been prepared to take your next big step.

✦ As you become certain of the path you're on, and the person you are, begin to appreciate other people's gifts, as well as your own. Each of us is exactly where we need to be and is no better or worse off than anyone else.

✦ When you don't live true to your dream, just notice what happened, learn from it, congratulate yourself on what you've learned, and move on.

✦ Your rate of progress will be fastest if you don't allow yourself to spend time focusing on limiting or negative thoughts. Keep choosing the positive point of view.

✦ One concrete step taken in the right direction will take you far. Keep your attention focused on realizing your dream, and avoid becoming distracted or going off on tangents.

✦ Practice makes permanent. Practice continually asking yourself, "Am I living my dream in this moment? What more could I be doing?"

STEPS TO PREPARE

The following steps will prepare you for beginning your dreamwork:

Get Ready

Purchase *The Live Your Dream Workbook* and a loose-leaf notebook or bound journal to use for your Dream Journal. You will be recording many of your thoughts and feelings during the coming weeks, so be certain to select a journal that you will enjoy writing in.

Also, purchase a daily schedule book. Look for one that can be used to record and plan your days hour by hour.

Get Set

Starting now, do the following *every day:*

✦ *Visualize.* At the beginning of each day, spend a few minutes previewing your day. What do you want out of your day? Picture yourself going through the day. What will you accomplish? What needs to be taken care of? What will you do for yourself? Visualize yourself living true to your dream. See that dream as if it were manifested already. What will you do today to advance your dream?

✦ *Schedule your day.* At the top of your daily schedule write, "The dream steps I want to focus on today are…." Write all the dream steps you intend to achieve. Then set up a schedule for your time that will enable you to accomplish these steps.

At the end of each day before you go to bed, look over your schedule. Write in your Dream Journal to evaluate and discover, "What I learned today is…." You become the person you want to be by first saying what you will do, then observing whether you did it or not. Your major discovery or accomplishment for one day may be simply noting that you did not follow through with what you had intended. Be sure to write that down. Do you want to put it on tomorrow's list?

✦ *Start your Dream Journal.* Write to yourself in it every day. Use it to keep track of your assignments and your progress. Get into the habit of using it as a daily log of "where I am today." You never need to show your Dream Journal to anyone, so don't worry about people criticizing or evaluating what you write. Just write for yourself alone. Always date your work. When you complete each entry, reread it and write a short summary statement.

✦ *Start writing in The Live Your Dream Workbook.* The exercises in the workbook will reinforce and enhance your learning. By simply giving honest answers to the workbook questions, you will be gaining clarity as well as having a tangible record of the journey you have undertaken. By documenting and defining your dream, you are able to look back and reflect on your progress, identify where you wandered off tract in addition to the changes to your dream as you grow, become more aware and evolve.

✦ *Team up with a dream partner.* I highly recommend teaming up with a partner to work with through the process of "Live Your Dream" discovery. Your partner will also be working independently on his or her own dream, and you can support and encourage each other as you progress through the exercises. Telephone your partner at least five days every week and ask each other empowering questions, such as "What dream step did you take today?" and "How are you living your dream?" Communicate your successes and all your learning. Emphasize the growth as you support and empower each other.

◆ *Learn, research, explore, discover, and welcome every opportunity to grow and change.* Read books, research on-line, and listen to tapes and discs that will expand your awareness and support you in living your dream. Emmet Fox in *The Mental Equivalent* states the following:

◆ Whatever enters into your life is but the material expression of some belief in your mind.

◆ Management of your thinking is the key to management of your destiny.

◆ If you want to change your life, *you must change your thought and keep it changed.*

◆ A list of suggested readings is provided at the back of this book to help you begin redirecting your thinking. Also begin the habit of writing the titles of books, tapes, movies, etc., that are inspiring you to renew, redefine and reinvent yourself in your journal and workbook.

Using these tools on a regular and consistent basis, you will notice your life becoming an adventure, with you in charge of creating it. You will become your own teacher, your own life planner, and your own masterful leader.

Now, begin!

VISUALIZE YOUR DREAM

Arrange a time when you can be uninterrupted for at least an hour to concentrate your attention on defining your dream.

Prepare for this exercise by putting your Dream Journal and *The Live Your Dream Workbook* close by. (When you are finished recording, and then listening to the visualization, you will want to be able to recapture your experience by writing in your journal and filling in the blanks in the workbook.) Set up a tape recorder and make yourself as comfortable as you can possibly be.

Read the following section slowly into a tape recorder, so that later you can listen to it with your eyes closed. When you're ready, begin.

Find a comfortable and quiet place to sit and start visualizing your dream. (Pause.) What *is* your dream? Begin to picture some ideas about it. Allow vivid images to flow into your imagination. Create your ideal scene, no matter how crazy or unrealistic it might seem. You can sort out and evaluate your ideas later. For now, just let them flow freely.

Suppose that, for the first time in your life, you have been given the opportunity to start anew, knowing everything in your life from now on will support you in living your dream. See yourself walking down a narrow path lined on both sides by flowers and hanging vines. You are enchanted by the beauty all around you. Floral fragrances fill the air and brilliant-colored birds swoop and sing. Breathe in deeply and soak up the warm, soothing rays of the sun.

Continue along the path until you come upon a scene that you recognize as your ideal place to be in all of nature. Here you are free of all distractions and responsibilities. Take a good look around you. What do you see? Are there mountains, trees, water, flowers, grassy fields, the desert, the ocean, birds, and is there sunshine or rain? Note the colors and details of this place, as an artist would.

Where are you? What is it you love about the particular place you find yourself in? How does it feel to be there? What is the one quality of the scene you would want to take with you wherever you go? Relax, and soak up enough of this feeling to last for a lifetime.

Now, you feel eager to know what lies just ahead. Gather yourself up and turn your eyes toward a sparkling light not far away. With a springing step, start out across the short stretch to find out what could be reflecting in the sunbeams so brightly.

And just look! There it is: your dream house, perfect in every way. It is in the exact location you would choose. Walk slowly up to it, noticing every exterior detail. What kind of house is it? Embrace and enjoy what you see.

Now walk up to the front door, open it, and walk into your dream home environment. Here are all the features in a house that make you happiest. Look all around, walking from room to room, exploring each space. Go ahead—open some of the cupboards and sit on the furniture

Stop for a moment to picture and relish what you see. What is important to you in this home? Where will you spend most of your time? What kinds of experiences will you choose to have there? How do these surroundings accommodate these purposes? What does the *dreamer* in you say you aspire to? Dream...and relax. Know as you imagine your dream home you are bringing the possibility to attract into your life any reality you are willing to commit and work to achieve. What are some of the possessions you desire? What personal things energize the dreamer in you?

Take in each detail of your ideal home to your complete satisfaction. Now once again look beyond, to see more of what is in store for you, to fulfill and complete your life. Begin to consider the central purpose for your life.

Imagine walking over to a comfortable chair in your dream living room. Sit down, and imagine yourself in the career position of your dreams. You are now ready and eager to make the contribution to the world that you came here to make. You are excited to begin using all your unique talents to do what you most enjoy doing.

See yourself involved in an activity you absolutely love to do. You can hardly believe you're being rewarded to have so much fun! What are you doing and accomplishing? What activities give you boundless energy and make you feel so good?

Think of the ways it is important for you to be expressing yourself. What is the gift deep within you that yearns to be expressed and given to others? What is the special understanding your unique experience has brought to you, that you want to offer for others' benefit?

How is your work important in the world? What profession do you most identify with? If your dream is to be your very best, perhaps you will delight in making your service personal—remembering individual preferences, offering single-minded attentiveness to your clients'/customers' needs, creating an atmosphere that lets them know they are cared for, joking or chatting with them, or lending a sympathetic ear. How are you making a difference by what you do?

In what ways does the contribution you make lift your whole field of endeavor to a higher level than anyone else has ever aspired to before? What things do you think of in a new way? What outstanding innovations do you make? What new ideas do you bring into reality? What improvements do you envision making in the world? What is your unique role as an actualized dreamer?

Suddenly you see yourself at a large gathering. Someone walks up to you with a microphone and asks you, "What do you absolutely know, right at this moment in your life, that makes you sure the dream you have envisioned is a possibility for your future?" You take the microphone confidently, and reply, "I know I will realize my dream because…!"

You release the microphone and make your way through a wildly applauding audience to your car. You relax for a moment, take a deep breath, and look at the interior to admire the car of your dreams. You turn on the ignition and glide onto the road to drive to work.

Soon you arrive at your ideal place of work. Even though you have a busy day planned you take a moment to look around and cherish what you see and feel. You love where are you and you acknowledge how the exterior space makes you feel. You open the door to your work world and once again sigh with satisfaction because everything is exactly what you wanted.

Your work brings you many rewards now, since you began living your dream. Remember the feelings you always wanted to have as you worked? What were they? Listen as I read this list of feeling words and remember those you want to experience in your work environment.

creative	enthusiastic	serene	inspired
successful	strong	invigorated	acknowledged
consistent	cheerful	satisfied	independent
valuable	in the spotlight	respected	reliable
responsible	capable	organized	confident
appreciated	fascinated	excited	powerful

Imagine yourself gaining the rich recognition you deserve for living true to yourself and your dreams. You know you are living a life of contribution and making a difference. What forms of acknowledgment do you receive for the valuable work you do? Imagine the one person you most want to appreciate your value. Who is this person? What is it you want him or her to know? How will you experience his or her acknowledgement?

Now imagine you have returned to your dream house. You find yourself settling into your dreaming chair again, feeling still more relaxed yet expectant. You look down and see something in your hand; you bring it up to take a closer look and see what appears to be a paycheck. You take a good look at this check. You smile as you note who issued it to you and see the dollar amount. This is truly a dream come true! You know you'll want to make a photocopy of this dream paycheck later to insert it in your Dream Journal. What fun it will be to have as a reminder of your commitment and to be receiving financial rewards for following your dreams.

All at once you realize you now need and want to create a new business card that represents the special qualities your dream work has to offer. You close your eyes to picture the design for your ultimate business card. You know the message must represent the new (dreamer) you. You ask yourself, *What colors, graphics, paper, do I want?* You know that later you'll want to draw a visual representation of it.

You look up and see the plaque hanging on the wall that you had made to signify your dream. You smile as you recall the process of deciding to make up a quote of your very own to hang on your wall. You knew that visitors would see it and instantly know what you're all about and would be enrolled to support you in living your dream.

You walk out into your garden and immediately become peaceful. You now know, beyond your work life, what feeling states you most treasure. You value love, enthusiasm, thrills, comfort, pride, peace, suspense, laughter, romance, awe, fantasy, relaxation, and spontaneity. You also realize that as you grow, change and become more aware some of these may alter and change. You may want to ask yourself which three words from your list are the most important to you. Then use these words to form a statement that captures your dream—one that will energize and inspire you each time you remember it.

You realize that you have been imagining your life and your future for so long that the sun has gone down. The first stars have come out to tease the darkness into laughter. Viewing the night sky with the same sense of wonder you had as a child, you declare your wish upon the first star, pausing to say, "Later, I'll write this wish down." Alone but not lonely, you feel a deep sense of satisfaction with your own identity. Finally, you have found the ideal relationship you always longed for—not in the form of a friend or a lover; rather, it is the relationship you have *with yourself.*

Imagine and hear beautiful music. As the melody enters through to your body and the rhythm starts your toes to tapping, you begin to sway and flow into a magical, carefree dance—fully feeling the *wholeness* of yourself.

It feels good to love and celebrate yourself in this marvelous way. You are certain *you are* the person who can make you happy. You are the one who will love and honor you always, unconditionally, no matter what. The person who knows how wonderful you are, how beautiful you are inside. This person thinks only the highest thoughts about you, knowing that you are worthy of nothing less. This person knows all your dark corners and hidden secrets, smiles tenderly and forgivingly at each lesson you have learned, and even embraces those that remain for you to learn.

Sitting down again, take a few moments to consider what you appreciate and like about yourself. What are your best qualities? What have you learned? Pretend you are being introduced as an honored guest at an intimate gathering of close friends. This person will sum up your most admirable qualities and character traits. Delight in this experience and know that you will recall hearing this introduction and smile at the memory.

Imagine loving and appreciating yourself in the way you wish a trusted companion would love you. Picture it: What would this person do and say? Imagine loving yourself in these ways. You treat yourself as something special. You do special things for yourself. You give yourself gifts. You anticipate your needs and provide for them, taking care of yourself with loving concern and affection. You love doing things to make you happy—not in a selfish way, but simply honoring yourself as an important and valuable being, worthy of the best you have to give. You have a new certainty that "My taking care of myself is best for others, too." You know that as you are well cared for, you are able to give generously out of your fullness, not reluctantly out of your emptiness. Pause to define the ways you now take loving care of your physical and mental well-being.

See yourself getting up and walking over to a mirror. Look into it for a minute. You see many things and focus on you, the dreamer. This dreamer—your highest self—is beautiful, whole, complete, and valuable, a person others love to be with. So alive. So vital and present. Look closely enough to see the star the world's been waiting for.

You now see yourself choosing to claim and create your dream. Others hear you saying, "I made a decision, and I'm going to do it. The truth is, I'm the only one in the world whose destiny is to live *my* dream. I'm it. Others may or may not join me, but even if no one does, I know what I must do. From now on, it's not excuses, but *results,* for me."

Now your needs are richly met, your life is full, you are fully self-reliant, and you choose to add another dimension. You feel naturally drawn to others who enhance and enrich your life. You move into relationships with other dreamers who are equally whole, complete, and satisfied with their lives. You and your dream partners in life come together to share each other's joys, successes, and stimulating times.

Your fellow dreamers are as enthusiastic about their dreams as you are about yours, and the joyfulness of your relationships is the sharing of your passion for life. Whenever you approach your partner, you read the invisible button he or she wears that says, "I'm living my dream. Ask me how!" Through constant updating on each other's dream status, you maintain your focus on success and movement and on what needs to happen to bring about your dreams.

The emphasis of your communication together always begins with energizing and empowering exchanges such as:

✦ *"This is what's making me celebrate; what's making you celebrate?"*

✦ *"These are my accomplishments; what are your accomplishments?"*

✦ *"This is what I think; what do you think?"*

✦ *"This is what I feel; what do you feel?"*

✦ *"This is what I learned this week; what have you learned recently?"*

Thus, you lift your level of communication away from whatever isn't working to what does work. You avoid bringing another problem to be resolved, another hurt to be atoned for, another apology required. You contribute meaningfully to the successful realization of each other's dreams.

You are now ready to see yourself in your dream leisure environment. This is your time for complete relaxation, rejuvenation, play, and fun. What activities are available here? What is the scenery like?

Who else is present? What sensations appeal to you? Are you quiet, active, working up a sweat, or reflecting? Do you laugh hard and play hard, or do you smile contentedly and calmly amuse yourself? How much time do you want to spend here? How often do you want to come to this place? Imagine returning home and displaying photographs of yourself pursuing your favorite leisure activities in a place where you can remember the value of recreation, rejuvenation, and relaxation in your life.

You have just spent time on a magical visit to renew your wishes, hopes, and dreams, and you know that you can return to this experience any time you'd like. Take a moment now and return to the room where you began. Take a deep breath and as you exhale begin to sense your body in the chair you are sitting in. Slowly open your eyes and look around you to once again return to the reality of your newly claimed self and to the adventure of living your dream.

Remember that the previous exercise is designed to stimulate you to visualize what living your dream would be like. Take all the time you need to write at length in your Dream Journal and workbook. Review all the thoughts and feelings that the visualization evoked by the questions in each area. Let your words create the stage for a vivid scene of you living your dream. Let your life's innermost desires arise to your conscious attention and form word-images on the paper before you. Truly allow that inner dream to come forth fully, projected into every dimension of your experience. See yourself learning, discovering, and celebrating every dream step taken. See yourself becoming your dream.

Ask yourself once again, *What is my dream? What do I want to accomplish in this lifetime? What do I want to be remembered for? What truly makes my heart sing? If I could do anything in the world I wanted, what would that be?* For now, set aside concerns about how impossible it might seem. Set aside the fear. You don't have to wait! You know what all your wishes, hopes, and dreams are! The time is *now*!

Zero In

When you decide to create a new dish, you have to know if you're going to make a cake or spaghetti. You have to decide what you want. You have to find out what the ingredients are, and then you have to get them and set everything up so you can make it successfully. You can't put in all flour and no eggs, and you probably can't bake it in the bathroom. You have to prepare the right set of conditions for making a cake. Otherwise, you might just turn up with soup or spaghetti instead!

Let's do some more direct, open-eye investigations into your dream to define it even more.

First, consider some questions. What did you dream of being, doing, and having when you were young? What was it about that idea that was so appealing? What were the *experiences* you dreamed of having?

What prize, award, or trophy won as a child meant the most to you? Why? What prize, award, or trophy would mean the most to you if you won it today? What would it mean, that you would value so much? Fame, success, applause, accomplishment—which is most important to you? What rewards do you find the most energizing?

Who do you admire? What qualities in that person do you value: charisma, courage, stamina, integrity? In what ways does this person represent your ideal?

One of the most powerful tools for coming to understand who *you* really are, underneath all the "shoulds" and "buts" and external influences, is paying conscious attention to what you do and think. Read the following list and, for the next three days, *notice* what is true for you:

+ Notice what your first thought is upon waking.

+ Notice, as you prepare for your day, whether you are excited about this day. Do you dread it? Is it "just another day"?

+ Notice your thinking. Are you a positive or a negative thinker? Do you look for the good or focus on the problem and whose fault it is?

+ Notice what the most important part of your day is.

+ Notice what it is that you willingly set aside everything else to do.

+ Notice whether money is a problem or a joy for you.

+ Notice whether your day is organized in a way that will lead you to feel satisfied at its end.

+ Notice the kinds of people you spend time with. Do you feel more alive around them? Or do you feel bored or drained?

+ Notice whom you're attracted to, and for what reasons.

+ Notice your surroundings. Do they support you in being your best?

+ Notice how you feel when someone asks you what work you do.

+ Notice whether you are most interested in money, security, or satisfaction. What do you work for?

◆ Notice whether spirituality is important to you. How much time do you give to it during the day? Do you live from a higher power? Do you put more energy into trusting, or doubting and worrying? Whom do you consider to be your authority?

◆ Notice how your body feels. Are you tense? Worn out? Energetic?

◆ Notice moments when you feel fully alive.

◆ Notice which activities move you to give nothing less than your best.

◆ Notice what you keep putting off.

◆ Notice where your passion lies. What creates real enthusiasm for you?

◆ Notice what you appreciate.

◆ Notice what you remembered; notice what you forgot.

◆ Notice who the main character is in your life.

◆ Notice when you give your power away.

◆ Notice what you pay attention to.

◆ Notice what makes your heart sing.

Notice if you notice, from one moment to the next. Do you pay attention to the feedback your feelings give you about what you are doing? What causes you to stop paying conscious attention?

A man from one of my workshops said, "I realized from noticing the way I felt about work that I had been blind to how deadening my job is. It was something I hadn't wanted to see, but my body had been telling me all along. It was so hard to get up in the morning! I don't want to feel this way for 25 more years, so I know I have to make a change. I want to feel warm and human in my work, as I do when I'm reading bedtime stories to the kids."

Another woman reported, "I thought I had no choice but to deny my feelings. It's the modern way—tough, but a necessity. But leaving my 2-year-old screaming, 'Mommy! Mommy!' as I drove off every morning felt wrenching. I knew in my heart I belonged at home with her, for now. Once I began really letting myself feel what I feel, I saw clearly that it's more important for me to be with my child than anything else! I'll find a way to live more cheaply and make that possible."

Until you notice what's real, you're stuck with it simmering below your level of awareness. Once you notice, the possibility of doing something about it becomes available to you. Use your Dream Journal to write about insights that dawn on you as you practice the habit of *noticing* in your life. What have you noticed? What does it mean? What now? Just as you keep important legal and academic records, this personal account will provide you with a record of your developing awareness. Important insights often slip away in time, lost forever. Your self-awareness will be enhanced as you look back over your writing and understand the progression of your evolving self.

I Would

Imagine you are looking back on your own life, nearing its end. Write a list called "I would." Are the simplest joys and pleasures missing from your life as it is today? What changes need to be made *before* it is too late? Write about this in your Dream Journal and workbook to summarize and capture your learning.

The Time Is Now

If you suddenly found out you had only a brief time left to live, what would you do? Would you spend your time differently from the way you've lived the last month? Would your priorities change? What would become more or less important to you? What would you want to experience more of or experience for the first time? Write your thoughts.

Your Dream in a Nutshell

Now it's time to go back and make sense of all the writing you've done so far. It is vital that you to develop a Dream Statement that captures the *essence* of the dream you will work on throughout the rest of this book, although your dream may evolve and change.

First, read everything you have written and highlight the most important ideas. Take notes, and then build your words into one clear, simple statement that expresses your dream.

Following are some sample Dream Statements from participants in my workshops. They may inspire and assist you in pinpointing your dream.

> *My dream is to write a highly successful book and become financially independent.*

> *My dream is to become a spiritual healer.*

My dream is to let go of the past and be open to new growth.

My dream is to assist people in relieving pain and maximizing their potential through the impact of my documentary films.

My dream, for now, is to be the world's most wonderful parent and raise my children to be beautiful, loving people.

My dream is to travel all over the world as an actor, making people laugh.

Your dream may be very different from any of those you just read. Whatever it is, it must come from the truth within you. Your own inner knowing is its only source.

Claim Your Dream

What is the dream you are claiming? Once you have identified your dream and written your Dream Statement, write it at the front of your Dream Journal. Are you excited, scared, or ready to tell the world? Start by calling and share it with your dream partner!

Dreamwork Checklist

Before you go on, review your writing in your Dream Journal and *The Live Your Dream Workbook*. To summarize your progress so far, write answers to the following questions:

❑   What have you learned from noticing?

❑   How can you be more gentle with yourself?

❑   Are you living parts of your dream already? How do you feel about your life in relation to your dream now?

❑   What concrete steps toward realizing and living your dream have you already taken?

❑   What have you learned from your reading and writing so far?

❑   What impact did the writing of your "I would" list have on you? What are your thoughts about what you wrote?

❑   How do you feel about living true to your dream so far?

❑   What is your ultimate dream? Say it over to yourself until it stays on the tip of your tongue. Stating your dream will soon seem like second nature to you.

❑   When what you are about is bigger than day-to-day trivialities, you wake up every day with a purpose. Now that you know your destination, you are really ready to live your dream.

ASK JOYCE!

Having a guide along when you are about to travel to new place is always reassuring, and often he or she can provide the needed information that will allow you to explore and adventure into new or unknown territories.

I am an expert guide and am inspired by questions, so I'm including a sampling at the end of the first six chapters I also highly recommend and encourage you to reach out to many experts as you live your dream.

Q: I have many dreams and wonder how many dreams should I concentrate on at one time?

A: The reason I gave my book *Live Your Dream* the subtitle *Discover and Achieve Your Live Purpose* is because I believe that once an individual identifies his or her life purpose a question such as yours is then answered.

    To begin to discover and rediscover your life purpose, I recommend that you make a list of everything you want to be, do, and have in this lifetime. After you gain more clarity, choose the dream that will enable you to realize not only your life purpose but also help you to create your plan to live true to yourself and your dreams.

Q: I have never considered myself to be a creative person. Can a person be creative and not know it?

A: Certainly! Just for fun, start saying an affirmative statement to yourself, such as:

    ✦ I am a very creative person.

    ✦ I fully embrace my creative self.

    ✦ I love solving my problems creatively.

    ✦ I awaken the creative genius that has been asleep within me.

Q: The idea that I could have feelings of passion for a dream seems far away from reality for me. What sort of suggestions do you have to rekindle this for the very non-passionate type person that I am?

A: To know the definition of the word *passion* will help you ignite your own. Passion is that feeling or emotion that is powerful and that can replace all other emotions and acts as a catalyst to empower you to seize upon and focus to realize a specific dream.

    Now, ask yourself, What do I feel passionate about? Do I choose to take action to follow and live my dream?

Q: I am blocked. I feel as though I am surrounded by brick walls instead of free open spaces in which to explore. What can I do?

A: One of the reasons that I recommend teaming up with a dream partner is to have the needed support when these "blocks" seem to appear.

Find someone to partner with to do the work together. (That old tried and true saying "strength in numbers" really does work.) Tell your partner what has worked in the past and ask him or her to ask you questions to discover an alternate path or possibly a whole new route for you to take.

Q: What if I do find my ultimate dream but I am afraid to claim it?

A: What a great question! And my answer is simply to get busy! Write a letter to someone you trust and whose opinions you value. Tell him or her what your dream is and how you are overcoming your difficulty in claiming your dream to alter your reality.

Q: I visited your Web site and started to fill in the forms to submit my own personal dream for your Dream Circle page. The blank that I sat and pondered for 15 minutes was preceded by the statement:

> *"The contribution I will be making to the word by claiming this dream is..."*

I realized I don't know the answer. What advice do you have for a dreamer like me?

A: I suspect you are thinking that whatever your dream is, its contribution to the world must be considerable, because aren't all dreams large? Well, they aren't, and you don't need anyone's permission to have a dream small in scope or dimension. If, say, your dream is to be in a modern dance troupe, what contribution would that bring to the world? Although it may not bring world peace, it will bring *you* peace and wholeness and joy. And if exploring the world of modern dance brings you into contact with new and different people, they are adding to your life as you add to their lives. Perhaps you will decide that although you will never be with a major dance company you will volunteer to teach modern dance at your local civic organization to young people, thus enriching both your life and the lives of others.

Don't limit yourself or your dreams by stumbling over what contribution your dream will bring to the world, but be sure to include any and all possibilities! Living true to your dream is not being self-centered. As you embrace and follow your dreams chances are you'll find yourself surrounded by others dreaming and growing.

Q: I am not sure that I really believe there is a seed of the dream(s) I had as a small child within me. Do you really believe this, or is this just hype?

A: We all believe what we want to believe, but to answer your question, yes, I do believe what you dreamed as a child holds a spot within you and aches to be released. Sometimes as we grow up we "put away childish things" and take on the trappings of sophistication and adulthood.

I advocate exploring what we cast off so quickly and incorporating it into our daily lives. No one is too old to revisit his or her dreams and make the decision to once again dream but also to attain those dreams.

Q: How can I make sure I retain a "lesson" or some learning? I have a tendency to keep repeating some behaviors that do and will stand in my way. Instead of living my dream, I seem to be stopping myself at every turn.

A: You are not alone. This is a common problem and one that can be dealt with and surmounted. When you set up your Dream Journal, place a divider in to include the lessons, insights, and learning you are discovering. Write to recapture the experiences and to document them, for future reference. When you actively write, you become much more aware of the patterns.

Do work with a dream partner or hire a dream coach so that by observing and critiquing yourself, you will learn to self-coach. This is a needed skill that will both build your self-confidence and affirm that you should celebrate every step of the way.

CHAPTER TWO

Clearing Away Obstructions to Be Clear About Your Dream

We are dominated by everything within which our self becomes identified. We can dominate, direct, and utilize everything from which we identify ourselves.

—Roberto Assagioli, *The Act of Will*

If you were inviting your best friend to come from far away and stay with you for a month, you would need to clear out a room and make space in your home. You might want to free up some time in your schedule. Previously important items and activities would be willingly set aside as you excitedly prepared to welcome your friend. Your friend's arrival might occupy a central place in your attention, as you formulated plans for your time together.

Your new dream requires adjustments in your old patterns in much the same way. In order to make room for a new dream in your life, the first step is to identify whatever interferes with your being able to live the way you really want to. You probably have some bad habits, such as worry or self-condemnation, that get in the way. On top of that, your spouse, your kids, the bills, the housework, or a broken-down car might make your dream seem unachievable. You may also have some beliefs that stop you. For example, your dream is to be a millionaire philanthropist, but you've never met a millionaire who wasn't an obsessed tyrant. With a belief such as that lurking in your mind, how could you become a millionaire yourself?

WHAT STANDS IN YOUR WAY?

Let's look more closely at the dream inhibitors in your life, those habits, beliefs, relationships, and distractions that block your path to realizing your dream. Here are four sentence-completion exercises. For each, number a page in your Dream Journal from one to 20 and write the specified sentence at the top. Read over this sample list, then, quickly and without pausing to evaluate your thoughts, write at least 20 different endings that apply to *you*.

Mindcleaning: Habits that Sabotage

A habit I allow to stand in the way of living my dream is:

1. Procrastinating.
2. Being disorganized.
3. Over-committing myself.
4. Not being totally honest.
5. Watching television.
6. Mindless eating.
7. Saying yes when I mean no.
8. Talking on the telephone too much.
9. Taking care of other people and not myself.
10. Allowing inertia to set in.
11. Not asserting myself.
12. Silently suffering.
13. Giving up too easily.
14. Being indecisive.
15. Being lazy.
16. Being irresponsible with money.
17. Not communicating when I don't like what someone says or does.
18. Taking on other people's problems and then resenting them.
19. Not preparing adequately.
20. Being overly perfectionistic.

Close your eyes and take a few minutes to consider your habits. When you're ready, begin writing.

Mindcleaning: Beliefs that Limit

If you believe you can't possibly live your dream on your own, without someone else changing or helping you, you're probably not living your dream right now. If you reason that, "No one in my family has ever been successful, so what chance do *I* have?" you probably aren't actively looking for every chance that might come along. If you see yourself as a failure, you probably aren't focusing on the possibility of being wildly successful. On the other hand, if you believe it is your destiny and your right to be tremendously successful, you have your eye set on that dream. We all choose our beliefs, consciously or unconsciously, and then give them the power to allow or prevent our dreams.

What beliefs do you have that get in the way of living your dream? Number another page from one to 20, and make a list of *beliefs* that stand in your way. Here are some examples:

A belief I allow to stand in the way of living my dream is that:

1. I'm not qualified; I don't know how; I'd have to have a college education.

2. It's too hard; I'd never have any fun if I worked as hard as my dream would require. I need to relax.

3. I have to wait until _____.

4. Someone else should take care of me.

5. I don't have what I need to get started.

6. I don't have a sharp-enough mind or memory.

7. It's too late to start all over; I'm too old.

8. I have to wait for inspiration to strike.

9. I can't afford it.

10. Something or someone else has to come first, before my dream.

11. I'm terrified of making the needed changes; I might jeopardize my marriage/other relationship.

12. I don't deserve to be *that* happy.

13. I might fail; I probably couldn't succeed anyway.

14. I can't do it in *this* weather.

15. I'm waiting to be "discovered."

16. If I had too much, I'd feel guilty about others who don't have enough.

17. I need to take a nap/get a snack/make a phone call first.

18. It's not what my parents want me to do.

19. I couldn't make as much money doing it.

20. I am a victim, and I can't change what others do to me.

Close your eyes and take a few minutes to consider your beliefs. When you're ready, begin writing.

Mindcleaning: Relationships that Deplete

Not long ago I had made plans to attend a wedding reception, and then I found my schedule closing in. My husband cheerfully offered to go alone and make an explanation for my absence, and I thankfully agreed: "Only if you tell the truth."

"What's the truth?" he asked.

"That I'm making last-minute revisions to my book, and I'm under a tight deadline," I said.

He came home reporting that people had responded with "oohs" and "aahs" and a great deal of curiosity about my writing a book. My absence had taken on more significance than my presence probably would have. Making my dream a top priority with myself gave it increased validity in the world.

If family or outside obligations make your dream seem an impossibility, which particular people seem to be responsible for holding you back? Make a list of 20 *people* who stand in your way, such as these examples:

A *person 1 allow to stand in the way of living my dream is:*

1. My father.

2. My mother.

3. My friend Sally.

4. My children.

5. My ex-spouse.

6. My wife.

7. My husband.

8. My boss.

9. My landlord.

10. My in-laws.

11. My imposing neighbor.

12. The loan officer at my bank.

13. The state licensing board.

14. My employees.

15. My sister.

16. My brother.

17. My counselor.

18. My doctor.

19. The teacher who keeps giving me bad grades.

20. The mechanic who says my car needs expensive work.

Close your eyes and take a few minutes to consider your relationships. When you're ready, begin writing.

Mindcleaning—Distractions

"It's too expensive." "I had a flat tire." "I'm too tired." Things often seem to become insurmountable obstacles that prevent people from living their dream. List the *things* that stand in your way, such as the following:

A thing I allow to stand in the way of living my dream is:

1. Housework.

2. Taxes.

3. A lack of money.

4. The government.

5. No computer/exercise machine/other equipment.

6. Lead feet.

7. My past.

8. Debt.

9. Not having the right clothes.

10. My weight.

11. Fear.

12. Bad luck.

13. Health problems.

14. The weather.

15. Watching my favorite shows on television.

16. The ball game.

17. My body isn't in good enough shape.

18. A lack of opportunity.

19. An unreceptive market.

20. Feeling tired and overwhelmed.

Close your eyes and take a few minutes to consider the distractions you have identified. When you are ready, begin writing.

Congratulations! *You* are now the one who is aware and in charge of what stops your dream. You have just reclaimed the power to *allow* things to stand in your way—or *not* to allow them! You can now choose. Read over your answers. What common threads or themes do you notice? What does this suggest to you? What new decisions will you make?

A New Point of View

New Habits That Support Your Dream

Now, go back and reread those four lists again, this time from a new point of view. Assume that you no longer choose to allow your habits, beliefs, other people, or things to stand in your way.

Next to each habit you listed, write a new habit you can use to replace the old dream-defeating one. Here are a few examples:

Old Habit	New Habit
Mindless eating.	Conscious eating.
Talking on the telephone too much.	Turning on the answering machine when I need to concentrate on working.
Giving up too easily.	Being persistent and determined.
Being indecisive.	Staying focused.

New Beliefs That Empower Your Dream

Old Belief	New Belief
It's too late.	Now's the best time I've got; it's never too late, and I'm excited about changing.
I'm not qualified.	My experience qualifies me; I will get any necessary qualifications.
I can't afford it.	I can't afford not to.
I'm a victim.	I'm a powerful creator.

Relationships That Energize You

For each name on your list of people, write: The change I am making in relation to this person is that _____.
For example:

1. The change I am making in relation to my father is that I will take the initiative and *act,* instead of just *reacting.* I will communicate to clear up misunderstandings, stop blaming, and take responsibility for needed changes.

2. The change I am making in relation to my mother is that I own my own life, and I will no longer allow myself to be manipulated by guilt.

3. The change I am making in relation to my friend Sally is that I am now able to say no. I choose how to spend my time wisely.

Focus vs. Distractions

Examine each thing on your distractions list and determine what can be done to overcome the obstacle to living your dream. You might be able to get around a lack of money by finding an affordable way to live your dream by taking initial small steps that lie within your present means or by obtaining a loan. You might decide to erase the problem of debt by making a concentrated effort to pay off bills. If an unresolved issue from your past stands in the way of moving into the future, some counseling may be in order. Some items on the list, such as not having the right clothes, being overweight, or even having too much housework, could simply be crossed off or reprioritized if you decide they are not valid reasons to prevent you from living your dream. Write a solution next to each item on your distractions list.

You now have an outline of what you can do to clear away to make room for your dream. Review this information often to remind yourself to continue making the changes you pinpointed. Note that more than anything else, the most important things to clear away are those old, self-limiting ideas that inhibit your growth and the full expression of your magnificence. By changing those ideas, you change your relation to the habits, beliefs, people, and things you used to think were holding you back. When it comes right down to it, you and you alone hold the power to choose your life by choosing the ideas on which your actions are based. Don't give that power away! Ultimately, there's only one answer to the question of what's standing in my way: *me, myself, and I.*

GIVE YOUR DREAM PRIORITY TIME

Clearing out your time schedule is also a vital priority for living your dream. "Do you know how *busy* I am? I couldn't *possibly* take on one more activity!" is an exclamation I often hear from active, involved individuals. Even when we're not spending our time exactly as *we* would prefer, we commonly feel that the demands pressed upon us preclude our having much of any choice in the matter. But if taking a step to achieve our dream is a last priority in our daily plan, it will also be the least likely outcome of our day and our life.

If you go to a doctor or diet clinic for help in losing weight, you may be asked to keep a diary of your food intake. Only when you know what you are actually eating can you know what changes need to be made. The same is true of managing your time. It's important to begin keeping a record of how your time is spent. Once you have conducted a realistic assessment of the time available to you and the requirements made for your time, your options will be more apparent.

Become a Time Accountant

Begin by keeping a list of your activities during each of the seven days of one week. Write each activity in a column down the left side of a page, and write the days of the week across the top. Tally up the amount of time spent on each activity per day. Leave space for totals for the week on the right side. Your page might look something like the "Time Spent on Activities for a Week" chart on page 51.

When you have filled out this chart for one week, study it carefully. Are you surprised at what it reveals? What do you observe about the way you spend your time? What changes can you make to manage your time optimally? Make a list and summarize it in *The Live Your Dream Workbook*.

In observing small children at play, I have noticed, almost without exception, their innate tendency to dump out the whole toy box before beginning to interact with the toys. They knock all the blocks down before beginning to build something new. Children inherently know the importance of starting anew, from the empty box or the blank table, when they want to create something new, all their own.

Create Your Ideal Day

Your time is your creative medium of expression, just as the child's box of toys is. When you want to create a new set of priorities that highlights your dream, start like the small child with the blank table before you. Take a clean sheet of paper and write your Dream Statement across the top in large letters. Draw a chart where you can show activity time segments for an ideal day.

Time Spent on Activities for a Week

ACTIVITY	NUMBER OF HOURS							
	MON	TUES	WED	THURS	FRI	SAT	SUN	TOTAL
Sleep								
Personal Care								
Home Care								
Socializing								
Exercising								
Leisure								
Work/Job								
Shopping								
Family Time								
Eating								
Unproductive Time								
Renewal of Spirit								
Financial Planning								
Journaling								
Reading								
Dreamwork								
Other								

Decide which activities you want to accomplish each day. Begin by allocating set periods of time to work on your dream—periods that are unlikely to be interrupted by other demands. Many people find that rising earlier in the morning serves this purpose. One man, who had difficulty sleeping, decided to work on his dream every time he woke up at 2:00 a.m.! He was able to turn a problem into an opportunity. Once you have set aside times for pursuing your dream, list your other activities in time segments to represent the way you intend to spend your day. Combine optimal productivity with spaces for relaxation and rejuvenation. Plan a way to fit it all in. For an example, see the "Time Segments for an Ideal Day" chart that follows.

This single mother, whose dream is to be an interior designer, felt trapped by the many responsibilities of work and family. As she begins to plan an ideal schedule for herself, she writes her dream at the top of the list, and first fills in the hours her coursework and homework will require.

Time Segments for an Ideal Day

My all-natural, interior environments are in high demand everywhere.

ACTIVITY	WHEN?
Work at the office and commute (arrange to go in at 7:00 a.m. so I can get off at 3:00 p.m.)	
Interior design classes, three nights a week; homework three nights a week; rest and relax, one night a week	
Journal and reading	
Prepare and have dinner with the kids, catching up on their news and the events of their day	
Exercise and housework	
Morning preparations	
Recreation/leisure	
Quality time with my family	
Sleep	

She knows she will have to do some juggling and creatively manage her time, so she thinks of starting her workday early and combining tasks that can be handled simultaneously. Writing in her Dream Journal, reading and keeping up an exercise routine are all important to her, so she schedules time for these activities, knowing that her success will depend on maintaining her personal well-being. Of course, she wants to assure that her children receive the attention they need from her, and her plan accommodates this also. She realizes at this time she will have less leisure time, but already her mind is racing to figure new ways of saving minutes and consolidating tasks.

When you have drawn your chart and filled it in, experiment with it for a few days to see what adjustments are needed. The woman in the previous example may realize she has forgotten to allow time for driving her son to his dance class one afternoon a week. She may then decide to have dinner out that day or let her older child prepare the meal. Keep changing your chart until you have a plan that works.

Note that this approach is opposite from the one we typically use in our everyday lives. Cognizant of the day's requirements, we begin tackling one job after another, often in whatever order the most pressing problems appear. We hope eventually to get around to those inner priorities that we keep a secret, often even from ourselves—but somehow the day fills up with so many other things. Or perhaps our personal style is to do what we feel like doing first, leaving our obligations to be dealt with later. Our dream boils away on the back burner and is never handled in a responsible manner on a day-to-day basis. The planned approach, on the other hand, emphasizes putting first things—your dream—first.

Schedule Your Dream

Once you have completed the preceding two charts, you are ready to take charge of your time, and the following method is the most effective one I know for doing so. Begin by creating a weekly chart with a key activities list to fit your individual lifestyle. See the sample key list that follows this chart. What categories will you need to add? Which ones do not apply to you? Make any needed substitutions. Use the charts in *The Live Your Dream Workbook* or make copies of your blank chart, to use over the next four weeks.

You can use a set of colored pencils to color in each block of time according to the key that categorizes how the hours are spent. Use this chart each day to monitor your use of time. This requires careful attentiveness to the clock and to what you are doing, but it has been known to bring about powerful revelations to those who take the trouble to do it. What do you observe about your use of your time? Write your observations in your Dream Journal and workbook, listing any recommendations for modifying your future use of time.

SCHEDULING MY DREAM							
HOUR OF DAY	**MON**	**TUES**	**WED**	**THURS**	**FRI**	**SAT**	**SUN**
5:00–6:00 a.m.							
6:00–7:00							
7:00–8:00							
8:00–9:00							
9:00–10:00							
10:00–11:00							
11:00 a.m.–12:00 p.m.							
12:00–1:00 p.m.							
1:00–2:00							
2:00–3:00							
3:00–4:00							
4:00–5:00							
5:00–6:00							
6:00–7:00							
7:00–8:00							
8:00–9:00							
9:00–10:00							
10:00–11:00							
11:00 p.m.–12:00 a.m.							
12:00–1:00							
1:00–2:00							
2:00–3:00							
3:00–4:00							
4:00–5:00							

SAMPLE KEY	
COLOR	**ACTIVITY**
Dark blue	Sleep
Yellow	Personal care/grooming
Green	Garden/home
Gold	Socializing
Rose	Exercising
Gray	Leisure/recreation
Pink	Work/job
Black	Shopping
Light blue	Family time
Orange	Eating
Red	Unproductive time/gossiping/etc.
Yellow-green	Renewal of spirit/meditation
Purple	Financial planning/paying bills/etc.
Brown	Journaling
Fuchsia	Reading
Aqua	Dreamwork/Living my dream
Lavender	Driving time
White	Entertainment (movies, plays, etc.)

Recently, I noticed I was becoming increasingly exasperated at my own seeming lack of time to do the things I wanted to do. Having taught the systematic inventory of time allocation for several years, I decided once again to begin using it myself. I was doing a job that required many phone calls and the management of complicated arrangements. I was being paid to do it, so why was I feeling so frustrated? I was not too astonished to learn that the job was taking far more time than I had thought.

"If I focused that much time on things I love and things I want to bring into reality," I reasoned, "I would be loving each day and bringing those things into reality." With this information in hand, I immediately made a choice: to resign from the position.

Others have also received valuable insights:

I can see that quality time with my husband is almost nonexistent.

✧

I am faced with the reality that a large part of my time is spent doing favors for friends and relatives—things I didn't really want to be involved in at all. But I rationalized that they wouldn't take that much time!

✧

I was just sitting down to watch television when I realized, "How can I let myself get away with watching television for six hours when I say I want to be a famous writer?"

✧

I realized how little time I'm actually putting into living my dream.

✧

There's no time for play and fun here! No wonder I'm beginning to feel burned out.

✧

I became much more conscious about the choices I make that affect the way my time is distributed.

✧

Part of my dream is to be an excellent parent. Before, I had felt a little resentful of all the time I spent helping the kids with their homework, cooking good meals, even going for counseling. But when I began to categorize these activities as part of my dream, I realized how much fulfillment they offer. It brings me great pleasure to be succeeding at what I have declared I want.

✧

I found out I fool myself about my "work efficiency."

✧

I've been neglecting to set aside any time for *myself!*

People often discover they could take more responsibility to manage their time efficiently. Designing your dream schedule can put you back in the driver's seat of your own day. Whenever I find myself doing something I don't like, I stop to ask myself, "Is this part of living my dream?" If not, I begin working to change it. I may stop doing it, figure out another way of getting it done, or make it part of living my dream. If it is something that has to be done to prepare for living my dream, I am happier knowing that I am on track.

If you are serious about living your dream, rearranging your time may be a necessity. Is your dream any less important than those of other great leaders who use every resource available to accomplish what they envision?

How do you feel about your use of your time? Is most of your time spent doing what is most important to you? Are you beginning your day by writing a statement about what you intend to accomplish? Are you ending your day by following up on it, noting which of your intentions were actually accomplished, and congratulating yourself on them? Does your time chart match your dream? Is your allocation of your time consistent with your commitment to living your dream? Define any changes you intend to make, keeping in mind this old adage: You love the life you live, when you live the life you love.

PUT YOUR DREAM INTO PICTURES

When you choose to have something new in your life—a new wardrobe, car, house, and so on—it takes time, energy, and work to get it. Time and energy are needed to find the items you want and buy them. It takes even more work to keep things in good condition for continued use and beauty.

It is the same with a dream: In order to have your dream *work,* you will need to do some dreamwork.

Now that you have cleared away many of the obstacles to living your dream, the most important thing you can do next is to become very clear about what your dream will look like. It is time to create a Dream Board— a symbolic visual representation of your dream.

Create a Dream Board

When I was teaching school, my students loved the assignment to create a collage of pictures of all the things that represented who they were. One fifth-grader cut out pictures with powder-soft colors, ribbons, ruffles, and lace. When she held her creation up to show, she exclaimed, "Yeah! That's who I am!" It strengthened her pride in her own femininity. Once the students identified in their minds *who* they were, a focus and sense of purpose came. They stepped more surely. Their self-esteem was renewed from within, no longer dependent upon comparisons with anyone else.

The idea was always so valuable with these students that I adapted it as an inspirational aid for adults who wanted to live their dreams. Dream Boards soon became a vital part of the "Live Your Dream" process. This is an extremely valuable project. As it takes form, you will begin to treasure the clarity you are gaining and take into your consciousness what your newly claimed dream life will be! Your Dream Board will take you one step further, beyond who you are now to what you could become.

Look through magazines and cut out pictures and words that portray your dream. (You may prefer to do your own drawings and designs.) As you begin, ask yourself questions to help you decide what to include. Do you want to "picture" your entire dream life or start off with a dream step you know want to achieve? When it's time to arrange these, be as imaginative and creative as you want to be! Participants in the workshops have had great fun by covering up boxes, which then became works of art in their living rooms and offices. Some preferred to glue onto a piece of poster board to create a representation of their dreams to pin up on their bulletin board and then made a smaller version to insert into their Dream Journal. Just imagine Dream mobiles, posters of all sizes and shapes, and so forth decorating every home, office, and classroom around the world. Dreams would be one of the topics of the day! What fun, what joy! So be sure to include all the aspects of your life: your accomplishments, ideal body, family, friends, relationship, home, car, work, finances, leisure activities, vacations—anything and everything that's important to you.

All around us, ads and commercials lure us to identify ourselves with slender, fit bodies leaning against newly purchased sports cars, reclining in fantasy dream homes, and lounging with adoring partners on luxury ocean liners or pristine tropical beaches. Commercial advertising is predicated on the powerful effectiveness of such images to get us to bring these desirable experiences into our lives. In creating your Dream Board, you are designing your own ad and picturing your own perfect life. Be as creative as you like, but follow one rule: You can only paste in a picture when you are willing to take the action required to make it a reality. Be sure that the images you select belong to *you*—don't borrow ideas from someone whose dreams and values differ from yours. Many popular phrases from advertising can be adapted to serve your purposes. One person used an ad for dog food: "It's time for Fit & Trim." Another chose the army slogan: "Be all that you can be." Yet another added, "The sky's the limit," but someone else in the class responded, "That's too limiting for me!"

During a workshop, a woman named Anna reported that she had started to attach a photo of a "picture-perfect model house." Then she stopped. "That's something *other* people want," she realized. "It's not important to *me*. I like the house I have."

Sample Dream Board
Words and Pictures #1

Sample Dream Board
Words and Pictures #2

Sample Dream Board
Words and Pictures #3

Joel, a maintenance engineer, said, "I come from a pretty limited background—negative, inhibited. If I were to show this Dream Board to anyone I grew up with, they'd probably say, 'Well, who do you think *you* are, anyway?' But this gives me the first glimpse I've ever really had of what I could become! And every time I look at it, I think, *Sure! Why not me, too! I can do that!"*

Joan, a successful businesswoman, said, "Two weeks ago, I made a Dream Board with an ideal house that was light and airy, and a beautiful pool surrounded by greenery. Today, I signed the papers on that house!"

When you finish your Dream Board, display it in a prominent place where it can remind you often and reinforce where you're headed. You have now declared your dream. And when you declare, life supports you and conditions around you begin moving into place to make your dream a reality. The movement may be subtle at first, but watch for each little sign of it. *Record these* in your Dream Journal and workbook as documentation of building momentum.

Talk to Yourself

In addition, begin having conversations with yourself in the mirror. Imagine your dream as a reality, and talk to yourself about it. If it feels silly to do this, note that part of what you are working through is the sense of separation between where you are now and where you see yourself in your dream. Practice this daily as you are brushing your teeth, combing your hair, and preparing for a day of living your dream.

Use All the Support You Can Get!

Call your dream partner every day. Read your Dream Statement and a summary of your day's accomplishments. Ask questions and listen for responses that are congruent. Reinforce each other for the steps you're taking in doing your dream work.

You've made an important start. Are you planning your schedule? Stay with it! Acknowledge yourself for your successes. You're doing great!

Dreamwork Checklist

❑ *Visualize* your dream.

❑ Write answers in your Dream Journal to these questions:

✦ What are you learning by visualizing each morning?

✦ How do you go about it?

✦ Are there difficulties or resistances to overcome?

❑ Schedule and review your dream steps and progress each day.

❑ Complete all the writing exercises in the workbook and chart how you spend your time.

❑ Write a summary of what you learned by charting your time.

❑ Make a Dream Board and display it prominently.

❑ Hold conversations with your mirror image every morning.

❑ Read/listen to inspirational and helpful books/tapes/discs.

❑ Call your dream partner each day and ask:

✦ What did you do today to live your dream?

✦ What did you *notice* and learn from noticing?

✦ What actions have you taken today to realize your dream?

❑ Repeat and register for your partner what you heard. Use phrases such as, "I heard..."; "I'm not sure..."; and "Did you say . . .?"

❑ Confront your partner honestly when necessary. Write in your Dream Journal to record your learning and insights.

ASK JOYCE!

Q: I read your suggestion about talking into a mirror, but honestly, I feel like a fool. Will I really get results from doing this exercise? I keep hearing my mother in the back of my mind ("Stop looking at yourself in the mirror") and it seems a little unfocused to talk myself.

A: In Chapter 1, I encouraged you to begin *noticing* both yourself and your surroundings. This method/exercise is to invite you to learn and practice the habit of what I call *the art of observation*. Through noticing and the awareness the act of projecting who you are and can be begin.

    You may feel self-conscious—which is not feeling foolish—but that will pass. Notice how you look and what feelings surface when you say your dream statement. When you begin, you may say your dream statement with little conviction or trepidation. Try putting some power behind it and then look at yourself.

Q: When I read Chapter 2, I laughed and said to myself, "This may be what stops me." My entire life will have to be blown apart. Where do I start? Please don't tell me to start by clearing out and cleaning my garage. That will take a minimum of a year's work and I want to get started on my dream now.

A: Get a dream partner—right now—if you haven't already. Remember the saying *"misery loves company"*? Well, lighten the load (and your dream) by changing it to *"dreamers love company."* This will also be an excellent reminder to adapt your thinking and attitude to your ever-changing life.

    I am very sympathetic to the reaction my phrase "clearing out" has on people. It is a big one but a necessary one. Get started by clearing out a drawer or two, and write to me as you check items off your list.

Q: It was fairly easy for me to do the mindcleaning but I am having trouble reframing the old and coming out with new habits, beliefs, and so forth. What do you suggest?

A: You are not the first to face this dilemma, and it is a good dilemma to face. I have always liked the notion of *"change your mind, change your life."* And I have plenty of folks come back with *"easy to say, hard to do."*

    Yes, it may be hard at first, but the results are so rewarding you will be glad you did the work. Why not practice a fun exercise I recommend? Catch yourself living congruently with your newly claimed beliefs, habits, etc. Enroll everyone around you to join in the fun and laugh when you catch yourself *not* practicing and change quickly. Record all these times in your Dream Journal for lasting results.

Q: You seem as though you have a good sense of humor, so I will be forthright with this question. I have a family who firmly and steadfastly believes that following your dreams is totally irresponsible. Short of moving to a foreign country and not leaving a forwarding address or phone number, how can I possibly live my dream and not alienate my family?

A: Get clear, very clear. Nike put it best: *Just do it.*

 If you are waiting for your family's permission to follow your dreams you may be waiting a long, long time. Are they living your life or are you? I encourage you to let your family know that you love and appreciate them but that you are going to do the work and follow your dream(s) responsibly and into the future.

Q: My dream is to earn an income by doing what I love, and what I am good at: drawing. I am not scheduling my time to honor myself as an artist and to follow my dream. I am aware I am lagging on this but seem destined to always have time for everything else but my dream. Any ideas?

A: Reread the sentence: *Designing your dream schedule can put you back in the driver's seat of your own day.*

 The use of the word *schedule* can be overwhelming, so use another word instead, such as design. Review the use of your time and design a portion of your day or week to devote to your dream of drawing. This may be a difficult habit to pick up (and the easiest to drop), but the rewards are immense.

Q: I finished making my first Dream Board and I already want to change it. In fact, I ripped off one of the pictures when I realized I was lying to myself. Now my Dream Board looks tattered, and I wonder if my dream is too.

A: Start a new Dream Board, but keep your original one. If you are the sort who likes to reevaluate often (and I am the same way), you may want to make your next Dream Board the size that you can insert into a three-ring notebook. (I also often make a smaller version of my current Dream Board so I can include it in my daily schedule book. I see it often, and it is a constant reminder to me to stay focused on what I want to do, to be, and to have.)

Q: Why is it so important to have a dream partner?

A: It is a very real challenge to keep your dream alive. A partner makes the journey more fun but is also a support.

CHAPTER

THREE

A Winning Attitude

> *Within each of us lies the power of our consent to health
> and to sickness, to riches and to poverty, to freedom and to
> slavery. It is we who control these, and not another.*
>
> —Richard Bach, *Illusions*

*H*ave you ever found yourself in situations where you look around and wonder, *How did I ever get here?* The simple truth is that we participate, either knowingly or unknowingly, in the process of getting where we are. The more we observe that and pay attention, the more aware we become.

At times we all want to say, "Who, *me?* I had nothing to do with creating this mess! It just happened!" or "It was so-and-so's fault. There's nothing *I* could have done!" We feel absolutely powerless over the situation—as if we're helpless victims. The last thing we want to hear when we're all caught up in our "victim story" is anything about being accountable and responsible!

Yet it is assuming accountability that gives us power over our lives. The more we practice the habit of acting from a position of responsibility, the more effective we become as human beings, and the more successful we become as managers of our lives.

BE ACCOUNTABLE

Let's assume, just for the moment, that you are able to see yourself as responsible and accountable. This doesn't mean, of course, that you're in control of anyone else's experience. But for your own experience, no matter what the situation, let's assume that you take responsibility *(not blame, not fault, but responsibility!)*. Now let's try a switch in perspective. For example, instead of saying, "You really hurt my feelings when you criticized me like that," I could say, "I chose to let your criticism hurt me. I allowed you to be in charge of *my* feelings for a moment. I recognize your right to your opinions—I can either agree and learn from your criticism, or appreciate that your view may differ from mine. It's interesting that once again I notice that I've put someone else in charge of *my* feelings. I see what I can learn from this!"

Write Your Victim Story—and Turn It Around

Do some work in your Dream Journal. Draw a line down the center of a page, and write a title for the left-hand column: Victim Story; and for the right-hand column: Re-told from an Accountability standpoint. Think of a situation in which you felt like a victim. Write the story briefly, emphasizing how helpless you felt. Then use the adjacent space on the right to rewrite the event from the opposite point of view, emphasizing how your experience was caused, directly or indirectly, by various things you did. Explore thoroughly how your action (or inaction) contributed to the outcome of the situation. Do this for as many situations as you can in which you felt powerless in the hands of some other person or circumstance.

Victim Story	Retold from an Accountability Standpoint
I had just replaced the tape deck in this van. I parked in the lot outside where I work, in broad daylight. Someone broke in and stole it again! Can't you trust *anyone* these days? It makes me just sick.	Actually, I did know about the rash of burglaries in that lot lately. We were advised to use the protected lot across the street, but I was late for work, so I decided to take a chance. It's a hard lesson for me about learning to get up earlier. Maybe I'll buy some insurance now, too.
That husband of mine! He's got to go and buy whatever he wants, *now*! We haven't been able to save anything for the future. I'm at my wit's end!	Well, if the truth were known, the things we've bought had their appeal for me, too. I could have put my foot down and just said "no." Perhaps I could work with him to develop a plan for saving.
Those earaches I had when I was little were so painful! I would be in my bed, crying and crying but no one came to see what was the matter. My parents never really cared. I was so alone whenever I hurt!	Did I ever think of going to ask for help? Gosh, I think I was determined to keep my pain a secret—just so I could feel sorry for myself, or what? My parents probably had no idea. Even today I hesitate to ask for help. I need to work on this some more.

Now, go ahead and write your victim stories in your Dream Journal. You may find it valuable to summarize by writing in *The Live Your Dream Workbook* and repeating this exercise whenever you catch yourself feeling victimized, until there's no more victim left in you. When you're finished, reread your entries, and then go on to the next exercise.

THE CHILD AS PURE, UNRESTRICTED ENERGY

Sometimes before we can get up and move on, we must first examine where we are. So now do a little daydreaming. You may choose either to read the following section through first and then settle into your reverie, or to make a tape recording of it (reading very slowly) to guide you through the sequence of imaginings. When you're ready, get comfortable, close your eyes, and allow yourself to drift back in time.

Visualize the Child in You

Imagine yourself as a very small child, full of love, joy, playfulness, spontaneity, energy, laughter, and fun. You are without a care in the world, and you are so irresistibly cute! You skip down the street with your arms flying, feeling the breeze blow through your hair, whistling, yelling, or singing at the top of your voice. The world is your playground, put there expressly for your amusement, and you lavishly exercise dominion over all you see. You instruct the trees and flowers to grow and the houses to line up in a row. You wish on every star, you laugh with abandon, you scream when frightened, and you cry with unrestrained shrieks when you're hurt. Look carefully to observe this charming little child. What are you wearing? Where are you playing? What are the toys you treasure? What does your mother scold you for doing too wildly?

This little child is a dreamer, and it has never occurred to the child to question it. You capture any audience, and you adore attracting all the attention and admiration you can command. You perform with utter abandonment. Do you see yourself there? What is your favorite role to play? Look at your audience: a grandparent or uncle, perhaps, or friends. What response does your performance elicit from them? Do you make them laugh or clap or praise you? Or do you go for shock value, sly snickering, and feigned horror or fear? How powerful you feel, to have such a strong impact on all those big people!

You love to pretend. Pretending is magical; it can make you anything you want to be. Experience this child-self. What does this child love pretending to be? Are you the queen, the king, the beautiful fairy princess or invincible Superman? Are you the powerful giant, king of the mountain, the wicked witch, a lion tamer, a pirate on the high seas, a mysterious wandering gypsy, a flying trapeze artist, Merlin the magician, a race car driver, a comical clown, an adventurous explorer of outer space?

Which side do you want to be on: the cops or the robbers; the good guys or the bad guys, the peasants or the royalty, the caregivers or the children? Imagine you are there right now, playing the games you used to play. How do you feel? What costumes do you put on? What part do you play with other kids? What are your most pleasurable roles? And what is it about the experience that you relish so much? Recall a time when you felt:

✦ Powerful.

✦ Loving.

✦ Playful.

✦ Fully self-expressive.

✦ Productive.

✦ Fully nourished.

✦ Passionately alive.

✦ Responsible and important.

✦ Joyful.

What did each of these experiences mean to you? What conclusions did you draw from each of them at the time? Live with these questions for a few days. Sleep on them, and record your insights upon awakening.

The marvelous experiences you treasured as a child are still a part of you. But you may discover in them certain aspects of yourself that you put aside long ago, to become a "grown-up." Perhaps you overheard someone saying; "Oh, don't pay any attention to him; he's *crazy!*" and from then on you imprisoned that joyful, spontaneous, uninhibited part of yourself. Perhaps you encountered someone who had rigidly denied the feelings you were freely expressing. When this person reacted to you with shock and dismay, you concluded that it was unacceptable to be that way. Can you recall the first time you decided it was not okay to be who you are? What happened that made you decide you could no longer be that way?

Now consider further: Do you really need to maintain that decision to shut down your aliveness? What would happen if you dared to be the real you today? Which experiences and which qualities would you choose to reclaim?

These hidden resources within you—the parts of your aliveness that have been suppressed—are the atomic energy of your being. Splitting the atom of suppression will release the boundless power of your being. You will reconnect your outer reality with the inner driving force that impels you to express your best. You will operate from the conviction of being who you *must,* and that conviction will be the ballast that steadies you through the stormy challenges life blows your way.

What if you went around being spontaneous, joyful, loving, powerful, and expressive all the time? Would you be dangerous, or a happy, fulfilled, warm individual? How would you act if you *knew* you had nothing to lose? How outrageous would you be? Or, restated, how *will* you act, knowing you really do have nothing to lose? How outrageous *will* you be?

The following example of one workshop participant, John, shows how visualizing to create a new way of being works.

John was a serious, reserved, and extremely intellectual man whose hesitancy to make a decision or take action until he considered every piece of information had prevented him from taking advantage of several important opportunities in his career. After John completed the visualization he began awakening the childlike energies pent up inside him through the use of puppets. "Gladly" was the puppet personality who was unreservedly *glad* to have finally emerged. Gladly went around noticing everything as if for the first time, taking delight in flowers and freckles and frowns. There was nothing analytical or logical in Gladly; he responded instantly, and always from the point of view of the delighted participant. Everybody liked Gladly.

Gladly had a tiny mitten puppet he wore on *his* hand named Frankly. Frankly was playful, ready to fire off a spontaneous answer to any question without pausing to think. Frankly could be counted on to tell the truth as he saw it. He made everyone laugh.

When John entertained audiences with his puppets, dimensions of his personality were revealed that no one had ever suspected were there. He was lively, quick, funny, and intuitive. Gradually, by projecting his childlike energies into the puppet personalities, John began to integrate these qualities into his everyday life. He no longer felt rigid and constrained, and his sense of adventure soon overcame his former hesitancy. John came to feel so good about himself that he began seeking Frankly's ready advice on major decisions. More and more, he chose the "Gladly" and "Frankly" aspects of expression over his old compulsiveness. Whenever he did this, his life became more fun. People enjoyed his company, and finally he changed his career to pursue an artistic endeavor, something he had always wanted to do.

Freeing up your child-self is a choice that is always available to you. So let yourself go exploring into your own hidden dimensions. You may discover a vein of gold there waiting to be mined. Whenever you know it's time to renew and revitalize this child-spirit within you, do some writing in your Dream Journal and update your workbook. Each time you finish, write a single sentence that summarizes your insights.

No More Unfinished Business

In the last chapter, you began to work on clearing out old beliefs that were in the way. Now, to continue the clearing out and making new space for your dream, turn your attention to things in your life that are incomplete. If you haven't balanced your checkbook in three months or your garage is stacked with clutter from floor to ceiling, you may be unaware that your mental energy is tied up in those things. You simply put them out of your mind, and they don't bother you—although one of these days you do plan to do something about them.

The fact of the matter is that every situation left hanging subconsciously reduces the reserves of your mental energy. We often don't realize this until we clear out and handle the mess. Then how light and free we feel!

This phase of "Live Your Dream" was critical to the life changes a woman named Sara decided to make. Here is her story:

> I started in my garage, going through boxes and boxes of stuff. I would take everything out, consider where I could put it, and end up cramming it all back into the box. How do you unpack a box of stuff you don't even want? There were my ex-husband's trophies; after carrying them with me through four moves, I finally realized he must not want them!
>
> But what really hit me was looking through my house. I had accumulated generations of family heirlooms and hundreds of valuable antiques. All these things needed a home! I realized I had designed my life around having a place for all this stuff. It was not part of my dream. But I had made it a part of my reality.
>
> What I really want, after all these years of respectable responsibility, is to be a free spirit. Now that I can do whatever I like, I want to be a gypsy! I want to pick up and go on impulse to new places. I want to travel all over the world, without a schedule or a return reservation home.
>
> I knew I had to let the stuff go. You can't be a gypsy with an antique hutch. It just won't fit into a backpack!

Sara proceeded to invite everyone in the workshop to a garage sale to end all garage sales. She sold everything she had and set off to live her dream. Now I never know where her next phone call will come from, because Sara is happily on her dream journey traveling all over the world.

Your clearing out may not be quite so comprehensive as Sara's, but your results, like hers, are sure to move you closer to living your dream. As you eliminate excess possessions, take care to remain true to yourself. If you love your old, threadbare bathrobe, you may choose to keep it and get rid of that newer one you never really cared for. Just keep your focus on identifying whatever stands in the way of living your dream—that's what needs to go.

Cleaning Centers

Here's an exercise to free all that powerful creative energy. Imagine that you are dividing your life into the following areas: work, leisure, physical body, home, relationships, finances, and self-development. Write each of these categories, spread around a blank page in your Dream Journal. Circle each in this way:

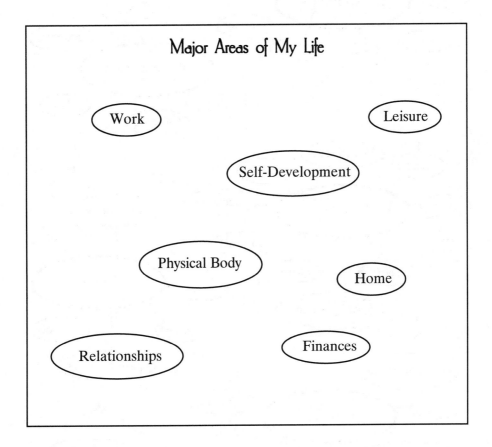

Major Areas of My Life

What would happen if you made an all-out spring-cleaning effort on your life? To enable you to clean out your life, clear up any leftover business, and launch your dream with fresh energy, begin by looking at each area you have circled in your Dream Journal.

You have created the beginning of a cluster diagram. Each circle represents a major category that encompasses related areas. Look at each circle and add subcategories to create a more complete picture of your life. Draw other circles branching out from each main category. See page 74 for an example.

Details of Each Area of My Life

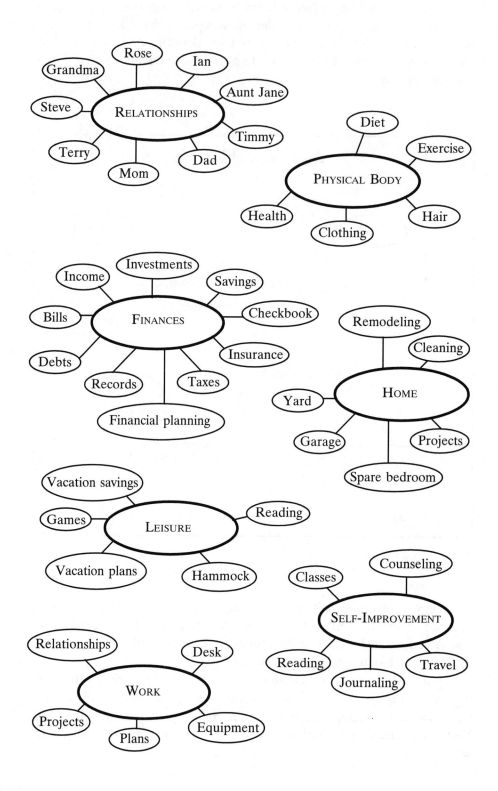

Continue expanding your diagram until each area of your life is represented.

Next, use the cluster diagram to create a "list" of all the things that need to be done to free you to live your dream. For each item on your diagram ask yourself, *What is incomplete in this area? What have I been intending to get done? What have I been putting off?* In your Dream Journal, write a to-do list for each of the seven categories in your cluster diagram. Write in your workbook to further integrate and enhance your learning.

Things to Complete

Be thorough and unflinching, now. Your lists may seem impossible to accomplish at first, but avoid the temptation to turn back, quit, or omit difficult items. Just pause to write candidly in your Dream Journal and workbook about what you are learning from your lists. Are you willing to complete things?

Here are some additional questions to guide you for each category. Use them to scrutinize each area of your life. Add to your To-Do lists and workbook whatever suggestions these questions bring to mind.

Physical Body/Image: What Needs to be Completed?

Stand in front of a mirror and examine your body and appearance. What actions do you want to take to make your body a reliable vehicle to support your dream plans? How is your hairstyle? Is your general appearance appropriate for someone who is living your dream? Do you need to lose a few pounds? What concrete actions will you take? When did you last have a physical exam? Have you been putting off dental work or medical treatment? How about an eye exam? Do you need new glasses? What skin care products or treatments are in order? How is your hearing?

Oh, yes, and about that exercise routine. What is your plan? How will you implement it and reward yourself when you carry through?

Are cigarettes or drinking a problem? How about joining a clinic or support group? Are there drugs you want to eliminate? Is it time to kick the sugar habit? How will you improve your diet? Specify concrete steps to take in your workbook and Dream Journal.

Now for the wardrobe. As you look in your closet and dresser drawers, what pleases you? What negative reactions do you have? Are you still saving clothes from a decade ago "just in case" those styles come back again? Would someone who is zooming into the future, living his or her dream, be hanging on to such relics of the past? Isn't it time to clean out all your closets and drawers? Plan to throw or give away anything you no longer wear.

What about mending, shoe repairs, laundry, and dry cleaning? Add specific tasks to your to-do list. What items need to be purchased to complete or enhance your wardrobe? Would someone representing your dream live in a wetsuit, a sarong, sweats, or some other type of clothing in order to feel best? Be sure everything you'll want to have is ready and waiting when you're heading out the door to live your dream.

Home/Yard: What Needs to be Completed?

Go through each room of your house and throw away or give away anything that is no longer used. What repairs are needed? What appliances need to be fixed or replaced? What maintenance work should be done? What remodeling projects are pending or necessary? Look around for borrowed items and return them, and retrieve items you have loaned out and now want back. Cancel subscriptions to magazines you never have time to read, and get rid of all those musty stacks of back issues you feel so guilty about neglecting. Do it, or hire someone to do it!

What about the exterior of the house, yard, and garden? Do windows, doors and locks need repair or replacement? Is it time to repaint? Do trees and bushes need to be trimmed? Have you been meaning to plant some fruit trees or flowers? What other yard work would you recommend if you were creating your ideal surroundings? Do it, or hire someone to do it for you.

While you're outside, take a look at your car(s). How does yours look? Is it clean? Do the trunk and glove compartment need to be straightened out? Is it due for waxing or new tires? What about routine service and maintenance? Do you have a regular service schedule, or do you need to make one? Are there repairs you've been putting off? What will it take to restore your car to perfect order? Should you be making arrangements to purchase a car? Remember that your car is an extension and a reflection of who you are and what you value.

Work: What Needs to be Completed?

What tasks at work have been left incomplete? Is your work schedule manageable? Is your office a mess? Do certain jobs seem to wait stacked up on your desk forever? When was the last time you cleaned out your files? How orderly is your desk?

What changes can you make at work to create an ideal place where you can live your dream? Have you been intending to ask for a raise or give yourself a raise? Are your travel and expense reimbursement forms up to date? What about other records you are responsible for keeping? What meetings need to be scheduled? What equipment needs repair? What improvements would you recommend?

What have you been wanting to communicate to yourself, your employer, your employees, or your coworkers? Are there any letters that could be written? Any dream plans or projects not yet put into motion? Make your plans to do these things now.

Relationships: What Needs to be Completed?

Consider each person on your cluster diagram. What truths have been left uncommunicated? What messages need to be delivered? What regrets, resentments, hurts, criticisms, and apologies have been withheld? What stands between you and this person? What prevents you from being completely open and honest with him or her? What keeps the two of you from meeting each other's eyes unguardedly?

What lies, half-truths, and withheld truths need to be cleaned up? What broken promises and agreements need to be acknowledged and resolved, either by keeping them or by making a new agreement?

What can you do to repair or resolve any damaged relationships? Do you need to forgive someone? What amends do you want to make if your actions have hurt or damaged someone else? Is there a relationship that has died or become injurious and needs to be ended?

What acknowledgments do you want to give to people who have made special contributions to your life? Make a list of letters you'll write, phone calls you'll make, and talks you'll have in person. Add these to your to-do list.

Finances: What Needs to be Completed?

Let's start with the basics. Is your current income enough, or do you need to find a way to increase it? What will you do? Is your checkbook balanced? Is your money being managed the way it will need to be managed when you are living your dream? There will be no time for interruptions from creditors and worrying about how to make ends meet then. Better get in practice right away: Plan a budget and stick to it. Pay all your bills. Contact everyone you owe money to and make arrangements you can keep to pay them. Also, collect any money that is owed to you or your company.

Are your tax records current? Do you owe any taxes? Do you need some help figuring or managing your taxes? Are your tax files organized and accessible? What else needs to be done to organize your financial records and bring them up to date?

What about security for the future? Perhaps a money-management class would be timely. When did you last review the coverage and rates on each of your insurance policies—health, auto, life, and homeowner's? Are updates in order? Have members of your household been informed about these policies and where they are kept? What about retirement and personal investment plans? What actions do you need to take to prepare for new dreams and your future?

Self-Development: What Needs to be Completed?

What are the ways you'd like to be improving yourself? Have you known for a long time that you might benefit from some personal counseling?

Now is the time to schedule it! Have you considered using a personal image consultant or having a make-up makeover? What about video feedback on your personal presentation? What personal and professional growth workshops and courses do you want to take?

Is it time to further your education? How about going back to school for a degree? Remember those other areas you always wanted to learn more about and skills you'd like to perfect. A class in swimming, guitar, tennis, drama, marketing, computer skills, Web site design, speech, cooking, religious instruction, and so forth might broaden your horizons.

What are the books you've been wanting to read? Have you made a list of them and gotten started yet? Plan a reading schedule. What about CDs, DVDs, and videos you want to rent or buy?

Leisure: What Needs to be Completed?

Are you making adequate time for leisure activities? What enjoyable ways of renewing and relaxing have you been putting off? What games or equipment do you want to purchase? What vacation plans do you want to arrange? What changes can you make in your home, work environment, and schedule to enable you to enjoy your leisure time more?

What kinds of recreation do you want more of? What people and places would you like to visit? What friends and family members would you enjoy spending more time with? What kinds of fun do you wish you had more of? What makes you laugh? What activities do you put off until vacation time that you could be enjoying now?

With the active schedule needed to live your dream, planning time for relaxation and fun is essential to balance work and play.

That's a lot to think about, and it may be a lot to do. Your completion lists may seem formidable at first. The best way of thinking is to see each completion as taking a dream step that will bring you closer to your dream. When you finish your to-do lists, go over them and project a date by which you will complete each item. Writing the date in the margin. Then throughout the next weeks, work on completing one step at a time. The more you do, the better you'll feel!

If there is something you are unable to complete immediately, figure out how long it will take before you can do it, and mark this date on your calendar. For example, if you want to have a new roof put on your house but aren't ready to do it just yet, write your targeted completion date on your calendar. This will clear your mind and your energy to focus on another step to take toward your dream.

Once you have completed long-term unfinished business, you will find that monthly maintenance is much simpler. Your life, like an automobile, will work best when you stick to a routine maintenance schedule, so get in the habit of handling and completing each task and each communication *right on the spot.* Review and update your completion lists regularly at the beginning of each month. Then when you sit down to design your schedule, you will be in charge.

As a participant in one of my workshops said, "Managing completions is like putting the tail on the kite: You're getting your dream ready to fly." People have achieved impressive results through identifying needed completions and freeing their time and energies to follow their dream. I joined in the learning and shared in the joy as I heard some of the following statements:

I found things I thought I'd lost.

✧

I made plenty of space to organize my stuff.

✧

I have the things I need at my fingertips.

✧

I can't believe how much better I look. The worry lines are gone!

✧

I'm not waking up in the middle of the night.

✧

I'm keeping my word and it feels just great.

✧

I freed my attention to focus on what I really want to do.

✧

I am healthier than I've ever been.

✧

I stopped berating myself for all the things I *hadn't* done.

✧

I let go of excess baggage I'd been dragging around.

✧

I was healed of some painful emotions I had buried.

✧

I restored my faith in myself. I am confident.

✧

I can look forward to new things.

✧

I have a ton of energy—more than I ever thought possible!

✧

I feel free and in charge.

✧

I am actually getting along better with everyone. It's amazing!

✧

I laugh more.

✧

I am living *my* dream!

✧◆✧

Beca, a workshop participant, achieved remarkable results through clearing out and completing things. Confronting the aspects of her life that were inconsistent with her dream was frightening to her, because it meant eliminating much of what she had grown comfortable with. Having been a successful financial planner and seminar leader for years, she had established herself in a predictable and orderly lifestyle. The only missing ingredient was the *life*.

When Beca examined where her real energy and enthusiasm lay, she found them in her love for dance and choreography! She finally understood why she was unable to tolerate music playing in her house: She *had* to deny that part of herself to remain a financial planner. Beca left her job, her old house, and many former relationships behind to start out anew. Now her teenage daughters complain that *she* is playing the music too loud. Beca is fully committed to making a new career for herself in the field she loves— a choice made possible only by her willingness to let go and clear out her attachments to a past that no longer suited her.

Give Yourself Credit

As you work on completing things, make a point of writing in your Dream Journal what you have accomplished and how it supports you in living your dream. Acknowledge yourself warmly. Put up a large piece of poster board and use it to brag about your completions. Tell them to someone who can be counted on to acknowledge you. Give yourself credit often for how good you feel about each burden lifted from your back. Have a party, and ask people to bring a list of things they have completed for the purpose of acknowledging and celebrating everyone's completions. Set up a system to ensure that you receive the rewards you deserve so your motivation to complete things will be constantly renewed.

Each month, write an entry in your Dream Journal beginning, "By cleaning out and completing, I _____ ." Your energy will be freed for greater and greater pursuits, once your focus is no longer diffused in so many directions.

YOUR ATTITUDE SETS YOU UP TO SUCCEED

When I was little, I was given a special gift by my mother. Every morning, she would come into my room and greet me with a hug and a cheerful, "Wake up! It's a beautiful day!" Some mornings she would modify that to, "Wake up! It's a beautiful *rainy* day." She was teaching me to live my life by anticipating and finding the beauty in every day—sunny or rainy. I grew up expecting my days to be beautiful. My mother's attitude spread joy all around her.

More than anything else, our attitude in approaching a task will determine our success or failure. *Our attitude toward life determines life's attitude toward us.* A friend of mine used to dread vacations, starting off each year's holiday already knowing that "vacations are invariably spoiled by rotten travel arrangements and quarreling kids. This one won't be any different. You come back more exhausted than before you started. You can't wait to get back to work, to rest up!" You might guess how his vacations typically turned out. One woman entered a workshop dubiously, saying, "I've done a lot of work on myself already, and I haven't seen many changes to show for it. I can't say I expect to get much out of this workshop, either." Once you make a statement such as this, you have an investment in proving your point. (Fortunately, later in the workshop this individual was able to make a gigantic leap in her awareness and move from intellectualizing to acting!)

Picture the person who starts out to lose weight by saying, "I've tried every health program there ever was, and nothing works. I've been fat all my life—it's just my cross to bear, I guess." This person is defeated before even beginning. Contrast this approach with a person who begins by asserting confidently, "I am a thin and healthy person weighing *125* pounds. I love eating this way!"

If you radiate an attitude of well-being and self-confidence, you will be well-off and self-confident. It all starts with choosing a winning attitude. Practice and consciously choose to create and live in a win-win world.

Look for the learning in every situation. Someone once said, "I never met a person I couldn't learn something from." Search for the learning. You will benefit where others merely complain.

Donna, a workshop participant, shared a time when she was inwardly agonizing as she was shown to her hotel room in a city 200 miles from her home. She had driven there to be present at her son's hearing. He had been arrested for narcotics possession, and she was angry at having to take time off, travel, rent a room, and chaperone her teen-age son until his appearance in court the following day. The bell captain interrupted her angry ruminations by asking if the fine young man with her was her son. When she replied *yes* to his question, he gave her a big smile and said, "You know, it must make you feel good every moment of your day that your son is with you to enjoy this fine city and spend time with you."

The man was right, Donna realized. "I was feeling so weighted down with these problems, I had forgotten my priorities. This stranger has brought me back to what's most important: my love for my son, and being with him to make sure he gets the help he needs." Donna told us she then turned her outlook on the entire experience from being pessimistic to optimistic.

Unloading the victim, freeing the inner child, completing unfinished business and looking for the learning are all important steps for building the attitude that will make your dream a reality. Adopting the following stances will further strengthen your winner's attitude.

BE COMMITTED

Do whatever you say you're going to do. You can't believe in yourself if you don't honor your own word! Your integrity is all important to one person in particular: *you.* You need to be able to trust that your resolve is not going to falter when the going gets tough and that you are determined to do whatever it takes to reach your wishes, hopes, and dreams.

STRIVE FOR EXCELLENCE IN ALL YOU DO

Stop for a minute to consider just what *excellence* means to you. In what one area of your life have you come closest to experiencing true excellence? How did this come about? What other experiences came close? Interview several people to get their ideas about the concept of excellence. Perhaps as a teenager you kept your very first car finely tuned and spotless. Maybe you have sewn a garment using only the finest of materials, and you painstakingly took out and redid each seam until it was perfect. It may be that you took on the job of refinishing some furniture, sanding and staining the piece until it looked as you envisioned it would. Have you ever gone over each crevice and corner of your home and office with a toothbrush until no speck of dirt remained? This is an assignment I sometimes give to enhance a person's awareness of excellence.

One man in a workshop shared his personal experience to elaborate upon this idea:

"Excellence is what you learn when you study the piano as a child. When you're first learning to play, you know just three notes, and all your pieces use only those notes. They are all in the key of C. Before long, you've learned the rest of the notes and you can play in several different time signatures as well. You learn the keys of F and C. Then one day you're playing along, and it occurs to you that it's not the struggle it used to be. You're playing well, and you feel good about it.

"Your pieces grow progressively more complex. You practice and practice, until you get every note just perfect—even the sharps or flats. Your teacher says, 'Good! Now let me hear it again with a crescendo here, and a slight ritardando in this measure.' It's a little difficult at first, thinking of all those things at once, but you manage. She says, 'Much better! Now you're ready to add the pedal here, and here, and notice these phrase markings? Try it like this!'

"You keep working, learning more and more complexities. You study stylistic variations, practice arpeggios and scales in five octaves and three kinds of minor keys. You build a repertory of sonatas and fugues, preludes and polonaises.

"One day, you sit down to play the concerto you've been working so hard on, and you forget about all those years of details—the music just flows forth from your heart through your fingers. You have transcended mastery and gone beyond to the ultimate point of it all—sheer, uninhibited, creative expression. The discipline was necessary; all that work had to be done first, to bring you to that point of pure excellence."

You may be fortunate enough to have had such an experience of excellence, too—maybe in one of the arts or in a field of sports. But I find it rare to meet someone who has actually pursued excellence to the extent of knowing it as an intimate friend. Yet, if your dream is a big dream, and if you want your life to work on the high level that you say you do, there's no way around doing the work it takes to get you there. Dreams are not about mediocrity.

What Is Excellence to You?

So now turn to your Dream Journal and take a half hour or more to write about your understanding of excellence. Then make a list of areas in which you will need to develop excellence to live your dream. Write what steps you will need to take, to achieve excellence in each area. Open *The Live Your Dream Workbook* and fill in all the spaces. Create a log of your experiences as you recommit and live to true to living a life in excellence.

Think of yourself as the person who is wildly successful in the areas you wish to be when you are living your dream. Will that success require excellence in specialized skills? In time-management or in managing people? In personal presentation? In communication skills? In typing or computers? In a foreign language? In accounting or in law? In managing your home and family optimally? Consider your particular needs for excellence as you write.

A fun-loving young man in a workshop I facilitated and designed titled "Your Life Is Your Choice" once challenged me when we started to discuss excellence. He stood up and cheerfully said, "I work in a stockroom here at the supply depot. It's always a mess there. You've got to be kidding if you think *this* place could be run on excellence!" I smiled and replied, "Well, I'm not sure about the whole place, but I do know that *you* could take responsibility for bringing excellence into *your* own experience." Russ good-humoredly took this on as his personal mission. He would come to each session with delight to report, "Did you see any trash in the hallway on your way into this room? Well, there sure was, before *I* came in early and picked it up!"

Russ began making dramatic entrances into the company lunchroom, announcing, "I'm here to clean this place up!" Soon others became more conscious about their surroundings. He put up a sign in his work area that said, "I'm taking care of my job—are you taking care of yours?"

"I got it!" he said. "It's about *me* creating it, myself!"

Ellen, another workshop participant, was, by choice, a full-time homemaker. Her top priority was creating a wonderful home that nourished, supported, and stimulated her family. Ellen had been a talented teacher in the past, and she made it her goal to achieve the same degree of excellence as a homemaker. Ellen loved participating in the learning process of her children, seeing them experience success after the hard, determined struggle, and awakening their delight in learning the intricate secrets of their world—such as the names of all the backyard birds and wildflowers in the woods and six original recipes using strawberries from the garden. Ellen's attitude of enthusiasm and excellence brought energy and joy to everyone who knew her and her children.

When you strive for excellence, you will inspire others, and it will give you zest and vitality to remain steady in the pursuit of your dream.

AFFIRMATIONS EMPOWER YOUR DREAM

A winning attitude often takes work to develop. An important part of this work involves forming positive statements about yourself to replace old, negative, self-defeating thoughts. As a baby, you happily went about doing what babies do: touching, tasting, exploring, and learning. You were without thoughts about what you could or couldn't do, so you tried many things. Very soon, a caretaking adult undoubtedly intervened with messages such as "Good boy!"; "What a bright girl!"; and "No, no—naughty." We accepted these statements unquestioningly.

Over time, as we hear such statements repeatedly, we develop beliefs about ourselves and begin to organize these beliefs into a belief system. Various experiences reinforce them and we begin to adapt our behavior to conform to them. If you were repeatedly praised as a bright child, you began to believe you *were* a bright child. Your young mind worked overtime, coming up with new ways to show how bright you were and to elicit further praise.

In the process of living that premise, your experience of yourself as bright broadened and took root. Soon there was no longer any question about it in your mind. You probably *still* think of yourself as a bright child, unless at some point that belief was challenged and you deliberately reevaluated it.

This is the way beliefs are formed and assimilated. As a child, it was a rather haphazard experience: Our beliefs about ourselves depended, to a great extent, on circumstances and the beliefs of others close to us. As adults, however, we have the power to originate beliefs of our own choice. We can replace negative, limiting beliefs about ourselves with freshly chosen alternatives. We can get rid of beliefs that don't support us. In fact, to live our dream fully, a new belief system that enables us to be our best is a necessity. Our old beliefs got us this far; new ones will take us into the future of our dream.

To adopt new beliefs, we can now systematically choose affirming statements and then consciously live in them. They will become increasingly true, until we are certain that that's who we are.

So begin by taking a closer look at the way affirmations are formed. An *affirmation* is a firm, positive sentence designed to convey a message from your conscious to your subconscious mind. It asserts something you know is true, even though it may not have manifested in your life yet. When the subconscious mind receives this message, it goes to work on a subconscious level to align with it and bring it about.

An effective affirmation must always be in first person (I) and in the present tense, and it must be stated positively, not negatively. So instead of saying, "I will not catch a cold and be sick tomorrow" (which would focus your mind on the idea of sickness), you could say, "I am radiantly healthy now. My body feels wonderful! I see myself performing beautifully in my dance recital." Now you have replaced the negative thought with a positive, colorful image. Because the mind can only hold one thought at a time, the thought of sickness is gone and your subconscious mind has grabbed hold of the healthy idea and has swung into action creating health.

The best affirmations are short and powerful—not wordy and intellectual. The intensity of the conviction and feeling in which they are spoken sets them in motion.

Create Your Own Affirmations to Empower Your Dream

Now create some self-empowering affirmations for your daily use. You will need at least 10 3″ x 5″ index cards. Begin by looking over your clearing-out exercises and other work in your Dream Journal so far. What positive statements do you want to focus on? Say, for example, that you realized that you allow your friends to stand in the way of your career (they distract you from doing your work). You might write an affirmation: "My friends lovingly support me in my successful career." Avoid saying, "Ben and Carla support me." It doesn't work to assume that your thought could control another person's behavior. If you are tired of fighting with your spouse, as another example, you might write not "Geneva stops fighting with me now," but rather "Peace and harmony pervade my home," or "My differences with others are resolved peacefully, so everyone wins," or even "Our love is stronger than our differences. Love finds a way."

Here are some sample affirmations that participants in my workshops created to energize and empower themselves:

+ I am happy, healthy, and terrific.
+ I am a dreamer.
+ I choose activities that support me in living my dream.
+ I am part of a loving family.
+ I am a millionaire!
+ I love what I do, and work makes me rich.
+ I earn, save, and contribute more money than I ever dreamed possible!
+ I bring forth the best in myself and others at all times.
+ I have my new job; it's wonderful, and I love it.
+ I live in a home of my dreams.
+ I take the steps necessary to handle whatever needs to be handled.
+ I am a naturally thin and healthy person.

✦ I *feel* what I am feeling, now!

✦ I know what I really want.

✦ I trust my feelings to help me make sound decisions.

✦ I am powerful.

✦ The next step for my highest expression in my life is visible and accessible to me now.

✦ I am honest in all my relationships.

✦ I live in an abundant universe.

✦ I am acknowledged for my fine work.

✦ I love sharing my sailboat and feel free as the wind.

✦ I live in joy.

✦ I am living my dream.

Write 10 affirmations of your own, each on a separate index card. Display them in a prominent place, such as on your mirror or refrigerator, or carry them with you, and say them out loud every morning and evening—with feeling. Imagine and visualize your affirmations as true for you. Practice focusing your mental energy on these truths, rather than on the way things might look to you before they manifest. Develop and solidify your belief in yourself at your best.

In summary, these are the basics of a winning attitude:

✦ Approach any challenge with self-confidence and a commitment to realize your dream.

✦ Look for the learning in every life experience, and find a way to benefit from your challenges and difficulties.

✦ Ask yourself, *What is the best I have to give?* Then give it.

✦ Choose integrity without exception—no question on this one.

✦ Commit to excellence.

✦ Work on your winning attitude using daily affirmations. Write your favorites in *The Live Your Dream Workbook.*

With your newly claimed winning attitude, you will become your own best motivator and your own dream coach. Your winning attitude can and will very likely make the difference between feeling overwhelmed and rising confidently to meet the challenges and greet the opportunities you must face along the road to your dream.

So have fun as you *catch yourself* living congruently with a winning attitude!

Dreamwork Checklist

☐ Teach the "victim" to take responsibility.

☐ Let the child in you come out to play.

☐ Be committed to completing things.

☐ Celebrate completion!

☐ Build a winning attitude of a dreamer.

☐ Read your affirmations each morning and night.

☐ Each day when you call your partner, reinforce each other's progress and completions. Share your accomplishments and whether you carried through with your scheduled plan.

☐ Keep up the mirror-image conversations every morning.

☐ Look at your Dream Board often. Add to it as your dreams grow.

☐ Continue visualizing twice daily. See yourself living your dream.

☐ Continue daily scheduling, recording your plan for each day and what your focus is each day, and note your learning and successes in carrying out your plan.

☐ Reread your writings in your Dream Journal and workbook often to reinforce your discoveries and learning.

ASK JOYCE!

Q: After reading the section about being accountable versus being a victim I realized I have rarely taken responsibility and almost always blamed others. I did the writing assignment you suggested and filled in the blanks in the workbook. What further suggestions can you give me to get rid of my victim-self forever?

A: Tell everyone around you that you want to rid yourself of your victim-self. Then ask them to lovingly suggest when the victim-self is showing up. I encourage my clients to give their victim-selves a playful title/name so it makes this change become more visible and heightens one's awareness. It often helps to lighten up the transition!

Q: You make it sound so easy to revisit the playful, joyful child within me. I don't really have a question; I just wanted to write and thank you. I did the visualization and the writing you suggested, and I am truly revitalized. Do you think people will notice this change in me?

A: Yes. My guess is that people will notice, and I am certain you will bring your child self out more often now. Enjoy the joy!

Q: I love the story about John and his puppets. Did you suggest he use puppets to awaken his "childlike energies"?

A: I sure did! When I was a teacher I used puppets a lot in my teaching. I found I had a "voice" inside of me that only came out when I had a puppet in my hand. My puppet could bring the children in my classes to a quick, silent space swiftly and hold their rapt attention for much longer that I could alone. It is a lovely memory I enjoy revisiting.

One dreamwork assignment that I have used for workshop participants has been to purchase a puppet that represents an aspect of themselves that they would like to develop or bring forth.

I have many wonderful memories of magicians, ducks, bears, eagles, frogs, clowns, and other "characters" talking and singing and performing.

You may enjoy having a puppet of your own to join you as you live your dream.

Q: I have written out 10 affirmations, as you suggested. Every time I read them I can hear a little voice saying, "Oh sure!" Should I change the wording to be more realistic? Some of my affirmations seem a little far out in comparison to my real life.

A: Do keep reading your affirmations and don't worry how "out there" they may appear. Your affirmations are just that—*yours*—no one else's.

Write down in your Dream Journal every time you feel the slightest "sign" that your inner voice is quieter or more accepting. If writing, reading and saying affirmations is a new experience for you, my best advice is to be patient and practice. New thoughts can be thought of in the same way as planting a garden: It will take time for growth and blooms to show.

Q: I have read the *Live Your Dream* book and I realize that although I am really happy doing the work I do, I may have a hidden dream within me. How do find this dream?

A: I can relate to your question. I loved teaching children and working with their parents. It was both a satisfying and rewarding career. But my self-awareness increased dramatically when I started taking workshops that were designed to stimulate and promote personal growth. I started to grow! I began to see glimpses of new dreams awakening within me and I wanted to pursue them, and I did!

I would suggest that you begin by living in your question. Start by adding a section to your Dream Journal. Label it "If I Could Do Anything for the Rest of My Life, It Would Be" and see where your writing takes you.

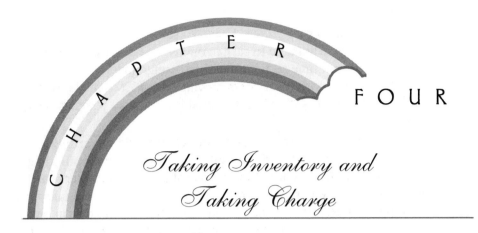

Taking Inventory and
Taking Charge

Destiny is not a matter of chance;
It is a matter of choice.
It is not a thing to be waited for;
It is a thing to be achieved.

—William Jennings Bryan

The ground has been prepared, the seed sown, and germinating just beneath the surface lies the beginning of your future. As the farmer, you are continuing to water that seed, nourish it, and protect it from disturbance or invasion in the vulnerable stages of its early development to ensure its hardy growth. You are cultivating your dream.

CRYSTALLIZE YOUR PROGRESS

Go back into your Dream Journal now to crystallize on paper the progress you have made. Read the following questions, then close your eyes and review your learning. Then, write thoughtful answers that sum up your experience with living your dream so far.

- ✦ What did I learn from creating my Dream Boards?

- ✦ What did I learn from working with my dream partner?

- ✦ What did I learn from writing in my Dream Journal and *The Live Your Dream Workbook*?

- ✦ What did I learn from my mirror-image conversations?

- ✦ What have I learned from my daily scheduling?

- ✦ What have I learned about the blockages I create in my life?

With these sorts of questions we can finally achieve peace with our past.

Nineteenth-century writer Elbert Hubbard said, "A failure is a man who has blundered but is not able to cash in on his experiences." Everyone experiences failure from time to time, but engrossing ourselves in the experience of failure only prevents us from moving beyond it to the learning. So as you begin the process of taking personal inventory of yourself, *look for the learning.*

In the next step of living your dream, you will have an opportunity to analyze your most basic characteristics and relate them to your unfolding dream. You can move from scheduling one day at a time to long-term and even lifetime planning. Where you want to go and how long it will take to get there is up to you. Remember that you are in charge. If your dream is to become a doctor, it may take more time to achieve than someone whose dream is to scale Mt. Everest. If your dream is "to tell the total truth," it may or may not take very long. Whatever your dream is, your process of self-actualizing can only occur to the extent that you *know* yourself.

YOUR VALUES

You behave in the world *as* your values. Your values are not something you can lie about. Your values are probably obvious to those around you, even if they remain undefined in your mind. They are the premise from which you operate. They are inherent in how you present yourself and in that which you aspire to and actually do.

What Do You Value? What Does Your Life Say?

Begin by looking at many dimensions of the topic of values. You can explore what your core values are and how your value system affects your ability to live your dream. Here's a survey to reveal what your *life* says you value. Take a few minutes to write brief answers in your Dream Journal and workbook to the following questions:

1. What do you find yourself doing most often?

2. How do you spend your time?

3. What do you talk about?

4. What do you do when you have a day off?

5. What offends your sense of justice and provokes indignation and outrage?

6. Which of your values are you the most proud of?

7. If you set out to select the values that would best help you realize your dream, what would they be?

I once opened a fortune cookie that read "Pay attention to what is *done,* not what is *said.*" This idea has stuck with me for years, making me increasingly aware of my own actions. I also began to realize that whatever I pay attention to is what is important to me. It is what I *actually* value, even though it may not always be what I *think* I value.

Here's an example: In walking through the grocery store, my hand reaches out and "autonomously" picks up a large bag of sour cream–flavored potato chips. I do want to be healthy, and I have been working at choosing low-calorie foods—really, I have—but the appeal is irresistible. At this point, what do I actually value?

You can develop conscious awareness by training yourself to observe your own actions and thought processes. At that point, you begin to re-claim the power of choice over your life. A person defines and redefines who he or she is by the choices he or she makes, minute-to-minute. And your choices are usually related to what you value.

Begin now to sort out and identify what your real values are. First, take a look at what you have always declared your values to be. Is there one overriding principle, such as integrity or loyalty to your friends, on which you would (and perhaps already did) stake your life and everything you own? Is there a line you would never step over, no matter what? How would you complete the sentence, "Under no condition would I ever _____."

Recovering alcoholics will say clearly what that line is for them: "I can-not take a single drink of alcohol, ever again." Survivors of Hitler's war camps have described finding themselves reduced to a single absolute truth: the only thing standing between them and death was their inner conviction of their own human dignity.

What is the closest you have come to confronting *your* ultimate truth? Have you faced the extreme test of what you stand for? If so, stop now to write about your conclusions in your Dream Journal and workbook. Our ultimate experiences often mark our strongest realizations about ourselves.

The answer to the question "What would I do in the extreme test?" may remain largely unknown to you if you have never actually come face-to-face with a life-threatening ordeal. You may have wondered idly whether you would command the strength of character to give up your seat in the lifeboat to a child or share your last precious drops of water if you were lost in a desert. But even if you are never put to the final test, knowing what ideals you aspire to is important in establishing your value system.

My favorite photograph of myself—the one that comes closest to pic-turing me as I love to think of myself—shows me as a 3-year-old with my hands thrown out, twirling in the wind. When I first started examining my values, I realized that self-expression was a top one for me. I could not live without the freedom to express. Relating this to my life, I knew I could not be in meetings where I was told to sit down and shut up. I could not operate in an oppressive system. I could not be around people who didn't appreciate my spontaneity.

By identifying self-expression as a top value, I saw that I would have to go back to school to learn to express myself in the best way possible. If I anticipated expressing myself on television, that would mean I'd want to present a thin, healthy image. So I'd have to get to work on that, too. If I woke up in the morning and thought, *I'm tired. Let's take the day off,* I might consult my values and receive in response, "You may not be able to do that, if you want to be out there expressing yourself—just press through the tiredness and keep going." So more and more, I make my choices out of my values. I monitor myself according to my values. Our values establish for us a strong, unwavering course to sail.

What Is Your Core Value?

Take your Dream Journal and workbook and explore as you write: What is the single most important value I stand for in my life? In what ways do I demonstrate this? What value is at the core of my reason for being? What concrete actions have I taken in the past week that show the importance I give to this value? How does this value fit into living my dream?

Throughout each day in smaller ways, our values receive countless tests. As with my tempting bag of potato chips, our small decisions add up to a major statement about what our real values are. What value statement have your decisions of the past five minutes made? If you have been busily reading this book and contemplating your values that would tell me that you take your own growth seriously and that you have a high level of commitment to living your dream. If your mind wandered and other intrusions entered in to claim your attention, what might that suggest?

Your Most Important Values: Are You True to Them?

Now list your most important values. (Note that the values you list are for right now; in 10 years, or even in 10 minutes, your values—and the priority you give to them—may change.) Write in your workbook and then copy your list onto a loose sheet of paper, and put it up in a place where you will notice it often in the coming week. For each action you take during the day, Ask yourself if you are living out of your values: *Am I getting dressed out of my values? Am I opening the refrigerator out of my values? Am I driving in this heavy traffic out of my values? Am I getting into bed out of my values?* Live in the question of which values you are choosing.

Log Your Value Choices

To really hone in on your daily value choices, keep a log for one week, noticing and writing about what your choices reveal about your values. At the end of the week, review what you have written and write a summary statement about what you learned. Have you crossed any values off your list? What work is needed to bring yourself into alignment with your values?

Are you excited yet? This work is powerful in its potential effects. You may be moved to question some very basic aspects of the life you have created for yourself. It may raise some discomfort, or even outright fear. If that happens, pay attention to it. What does it mean? What message is there for you? What will you choose to do?

Meaningful changes often come out of this work. A characteristic realization is, "My values haven't changed in years—maybe since I was born. I had never consciously sorted through them and made my own independent choices."

Only by living true to your values can you live true to yourself. Without values, your life will lack focus and clarity—as if you're lobbing a tennis ball back and forth across the net but not really playing tennis. With your values clearly in place, your tennis game has boundaries and rules, and you can score points and be penalized for faults. Hitting the ball assumes purpose and intention. You have an investment in the well-placed serve and the skillful return. You know when you're winning.

Socrates drank the hemlock to remain true to his values. Gandhi went to prison. Martin Luther King, Jr. died in the service of his values. Mother Teresa chose a life in poverty to honor her values. Perhaps the measure of our greatness lies in conforming our lives to the values we espouse.

The exercises that follow can help you discover more about the values that are most important to you.

Choosing and Re-choosing Your Values

Read over the list of values that follows, putting check marks next to those that are particularly important to you. Take your Dream Journal and copy down the values you have marked. Add to them to make your own list.

I value:

Integrity	Beauty	Companionship	Comfort
Meaningful work	Security	Balance	Service to others
Nature	Freedom	Power	Love
Intelligence	Inner peace	Self-discipline	Money
Learning	Spirituality	Wisdom	Power
Spontaneity	Fitness	Humor	Exercise
Simplicity	Competence	Order	Spirit
Relationships	Creativity	Excellence	Dreams
Health	Self-expression	Honesty	
		Economy	

Now go over your list and select the *five* most important values in your life as it is right now. Then, write to summarize in your workbook, explaining how you chose those five.

Next, consider what top five values you would choose if your most important priority were to bring your dream into reality. What would you need to value most highly to make your dream possible? Write another paragraph explaining these choices and discussing what changes you would make in your current lifestyle. When you have completed this work, review what you have recorded every day as you return to your regular daily activities.

Every Thought Counts

For the next 30 minutes, observe your thoughts. Keep a tally sheet, counting the number of thoughts you have that support the values you listed and the number that do not. Are you living out of the values your dream represents?

Make Your Own Honor Roll

Take five blank sheets of paper now and write one of your most important values on the top of each (as a heading). Tape these on a bulletin board, a wall, or the refrigerator. Over the next three days, consciously direct your attention to observing what your actual values are. Catch yourself making choices that agree with and support your values. Each time you do, list it on the corresponding page. At the end of the three-day period, spend some time with your Dream Journal and workbook writing what you have observed. A woman from one of my workshops said, "When I figured out the values I wanted to live by, I realized I had spent the last two days without ever giving them a thought! I want to be more cognizant of my choices." How did your lists turn out? Are your actions consistent with what you say you value? What have you learned about your values?

Strengthen a Value

This exercise can provide valuable input whenever you begin to feel off balance and out of harmony with yourself. Simply select one value to focus on, post your blank page, and begin listing what you do. Here's an example from a day's entries written by Nick, a young man who wanted to build his self-confidence by learning to manage everyday tasks and business opportunities more competently.

Competence
- ✦ Cleaned every speck of corrosion from around the bathroom faucets when I shaved—ultra-perfectionism!

- ✦ Read the camera manual, so I can feel competent about operating all the adjustments and know how to take the best picture under any circumstance.

✦ Took extra care changing the baby. No need to feel any doubt about my competence to do simple chores like that!

✦ Asked my client for a more detailed description of exactly what he wanted, then checked its availability through several outlets. Drew-up an exacting proposal outlining how we could optimally meet the client's needs at a competitive price.

✦ Cleaned off my desk. I'm on top of everything now.

✦ Fit in a brisk walk after lunch, so I would feel alert in the staff conference.

The attention he gave to recording these incidents went a long way toward increasing Nick's sense of being able to function competently in his world. Here's another list compiled by Nick several weeks later, when he decided that life had become too serious and he wanted more laughter and fun.

Humor

✦ Got some old *The Three Stooges* videos from the library.

✦ Read jokes to the kids at story time.

✦ Started spreading jokes among the crew at work.

✦ Got everybody around the office telling funny things that have happened to them.

✦ Started looking for something to laugh about in every serious situation.

✦ Went with Seri to an improvisational comedy theater where we laughed our heads off.

You can imagine that Nick's list, and putting his focus on the value of humor, helped him to feel less serious and laugh.

Live Your Values

Now use the information you have gathered about your values. For the next week, consciously choose to live according to your values. This may mean pausing just as you start to leap into a gossip session, by remembering your value of integrity. It may mean wiping away those crumbs and straightening up the mess instead of walking away from it, as you remember your value of neatness and order. It may mean forcing yourself to take a break from the job to relax and honor the value you place on leisure time or writing playtime into your busy work schedule.

Observe exactly what you do or don't do in accordance with your values. Observe your ideas, actions, and thoughts. Gloria identified intimacy, health, honesty, and service among her top values. She placed these foremost in her mind as she went through an entire week. The first thing she noticed was how often she entertained thoughts she was unwilling to share with her husband and how rarely she was open enough to tell him how she really felt. She began watching herself go through the rituals of play-acting intimacy, while simultaneously being aware that her mind was still revolving around the previous evening's conflict.

At this point, Gloria stopped to ask herself squarely, "Is intimacy really one of my top values? From what I'm doing, I wonder if it's not just the *appearance* of intimacy that I seek. Maybe I've been fooling myself about intimacy all along. Should I select another, truer value and stop pretending?"

Finally, she decided that intimacy really *was* important to her, and that she would have to be more honest with *herself,* as well as with her husband. Rather than censoring her ill-intentioned thoughts, then, Gloria began using their appearance to indicate moments when she needed to be more honest. She also realized that she had to respect her own feelings before she could be intimate with anyone else, and that sharing worries and angry feelings brings real intimacy—not play-acting the "perfect wife." Simultaneously, her health improved and her blood pressure went down. She found herself offering her service to the community in a lighter, more joyful spirit as well.

Communicate About Values

As Gloria's were, your values are also continuously evolving as your understanding grows. The first conflicts of young adults seeking independence from their parents often arise out of the questioning of values. Clashing value systems can leave lasting rifts between parent and child. If this is true for you, here's another valuable exercise: Go to your Dream Journal and write a dialogue between yourself and your mother and father on the subject of values. Try to appreciate their values, and explain your values to them. Tell them how your values have changed since you were a child. Work to arrive at each person's being able to accept the other's values, without needing to change them. Write a statement summarizing the acceptance you have achieved in *The Live Your Dream Workbook.*

During a workshop session, Kristina stated that her dream was to be a writer. In analyzing what it would take, she wrote to herself in her Dream Journal, "You say you want to be a writer. But whenever your husband comes in, you immediately shift your whole focus away from your work, onto meeting his expectations and needs. I'm beginning to see that the result of this self-betrayal is a lot of anger and tears." Kristina came to workshop reporting, "Before I looked at this, I was just depressed. I thought of suicide. I saw no other way out. Now, my desire to live true to myself is stronger than my impulse to give up."

Kristina began to select values that would support her success as a writer. She decided that to be self-employed she would have to value her own time at least as highly as any other employer would. As her own employer, she would expect herself to produce a reasonable quantity and quality of work. She would hold herself accountable for a specified number of hours per week on the job and a committed level of performance. Self-discipline would be important, along with assertiveness and improved communication with her husband. At the same time, she would need to value responsible management of her time, so that she could ensure at least one hour daily for reading and research, four hours a week for sending out manuscript queries, and at least two hours a day of quiet, uninterrupted solitude dedicated to pure creative thought.

Kristina was surprised to discover that her husband could get along quite well without her hovering solicitous attention and that he also was excited about helping her live her dream.

Deanne, another workshop participant, reported, "I've been saying all along that I value money, but I have resisted doing everything that would bring in money. I guess I wanted to believe I could value *spending* money without having to be responsible for *earning* it! Today, I got the usual invitations—'How about going to lunch?' etc., and you know what I said? I set aside my impulsive self that has been getting me in trouble and replied, 'I'd love to, but I've decided to start taking my value of making money more seriously. This work's got to get done. Thanks, anyway.' And I went right back to the job without a backward look!"

Bill had a successful law practice that he described modestly as "what I do for my income." Every spare minute he devoted to tending his exquisite orchid collection and to traveling. When he settled into defining what his values were, Bill began by exclaiming, "I'm a total hypocrite!" He was overwhelmed by the guilt he felt about the time he "wasted," "puttering around" in his garden.

In probing what he actually valued, Bill discovered, "I know what it is! It's *balance*. Gardening represents my creativity—the side of myself that I have to suppress during the long hours of poring over volumes of legal precedents and carrying out routine legal proceedings. It makes sense to incorporate balance into my life."

Value Your Dream

Have you identified what your *real* values are? Do you value your *dream?* Have you decided which values you need at the core of your commitment to live your dream? What are you going to need to value in order to live a dream like yours? Post these values prominently where you will notice them often. Write about ways you will demonstrate your values to the world. Noticing and recording your values on a continual basis will ensure that you continue to empower yourself to live your dream.

When you decide to go the full distance for your dream, know that your shift may take time. It may mean going back to school or going for personal counseling to clear away the blocks from your past. It may take setting three different alarm clocks around your house or buying an answering machine to screen your telephone calls. There is no easy way around the work that has to be done. What are the steps you need to take? Begin by defining them.

Reach Out and Ask

Reach out and ask for the help you need. Each day for a week, ask your dream partner to support you with questions such as, "How were you true to your values today?" and "How can you be true to your values tomorrow?" Actively practice living in congruence with what you value—today and every day.

STAYING MOTIVATED: TAKE CHARGE NOW!

In Chapter 1, we began to explore what your most powerful motivators are. Now let's take a look at two different kinds of motivation, to identify what characterizes the most potent motivators and then find out how motivators are related to our values.

In my experience as an educator, I continually noticed two different learning approaches among children in the classroom. One child will approach every project with a vitality that is self-nourishing and self-propelling; another will sit passively and wait, asking, "Teacher, now what do I do?" This child rarely takes the initiative, depends on others for direction, and waits to be told what to do next. When a project is completed, this child looks first to the teacher for rewards and approval, whereas the self-directed child obtains great satisfaction from completing the project successfully. The teacher's acknowledgment is almost superfluous to the self-motivated child. Both children may end up learning the same basic information, but the self-directed child has gained a boost in independence and self-esteem in the process; the outer-directed child has further reinforced his or her own dependency and feelings of inadequacy.

When your motivation comes from within, you are self-directed and self-fulfilling. Your efforts proceed with focus toward goals that bring their own inherent reinforcements. You may seek others' opinions, but you won't rely on their direction before you make any move of your own. You don't have to go to somebody else to find out, "Am I good enough?" Your sense of certainty comes from yourself, not from anyone else. You don't have to wait for your spouse to "let" you do what you choose as important for your own growth, or for your parents to finally give their approval of you, or for "permission" from your friends to set out in a direction you know is right for you. You, not someone else, are responsible for making the choices that bring your good to you.

Have you ever started down a cafeteria line knowing what you felt like eating, but then after you saw the special for the day and that super-appealing dessert, you ended up buying a meal that wasn't what you wanted at all? Did you notice how unsatisfying it was? The afterthought probably occurred to you, *Why didn't I trust my own intuition in the first place?*

When you go shopping for clothes, do you get a clear picture of what you want first, or do you find yourself purchasing whatever you see that is appealing or on sale and getting home without having found the one thing you especially needed? Do you keep your house clean because *you* like it clean, or because of someone else's opinions or expectations? Accomplishing the same task can bring, on the one hand, satisfaction and fulfillment or, on the other hand, powerlessness and resentment.

Outer-directed motivation is based on the need to be right, to gain approval, reward, or recognition from someone else, or on the fear of punishment or of commitment. Inner-directed motivation is based on a love for self and others, desire for the highest good for everyone concerned, a satisfaction in one's own accomplishments and learning, making a contribution for the sake of giving without expecting direct returns, and willingly assuming responsibility for creating the outcome you desire.

Where Does Your Motivation Come From?

Look over the values list you just completed. Which of your top five values involve inner-directed motivators? Which involve outer-directed motivators? What do you think about this? Write your thoughts in your Dream Journal and workbook.

Louise began looking at her top values by considering whether freedom was inner- or outer-directed. Basically, she thought, my desire for freedom comes from somewhere inside. My spirit soars when I feel free. I am creative, natural, and alive! I love the exhilaration of freedom, and I would do almost anything for it. I feel constricted when others impose their rules on me. If I am reacting against someone's trying to inhibit my freedom, I might misinterpret this as being outer-directed at the time, but afterward I would realize that my core commitment to freedom comes from within. Were it not for that, I'd have no basis for reacting at all. Freedom is a strong inner-directed motivator for me.

Looking next at another of her top values, Louise surprised herself by deciding that *sex,* for her, involved mainly outer-directed motivation. Sex was satisfying occasionally, but the main reason she had given it high priority on her values list was because through sex, she hoped to "earn" the approval she longed to receive for her physical body. Seeing this opened up a whole series of further realizations for Louise. She said, "No wonder my relationships with men seem to end before much of anything comes of them. I haven't been honest (another one of my values, incidentally!) with myself about what I really wanted: approval. And I have been asking men to give me something I could not give to myself: a sense of being approved of, physically. This actually counteracts my value of freedom, as well, because I could never feel really free as long as I was always out to buy approval with my body!" Louise decided to choose *approval* as an inner motivator, instead, and to direct her energy into actions that made her feel good about herself.

Redirect Your Motivation

What choices can you make to increase inner-directed motivation? Would you associate inner-directed motivation with selfishness or not? Write your thoughts about this also.

Choose and Re-choose Your Motivators

Read the following paragraph, and then close your eyes to imagine yourself in the scenario it portrays.

> The big day has finally arrived. You know that these last five years of training are about to pay off, as you are a top-ranked contender in the Boston Marathon today. Your training has been relentless, and you are completely ready now, eager for the race to begin. There it is— the call for the line-up! Events proceed from then on in a blur, with every cell in your body and brain focused on making the best move to keep on going strong, concentrating on the course, flying toward the finish line. Suddenly, in a roar of applause and a flash of bright lights and colors, it's over. You won! You put your ability to the supreme test, and victory is yours. As if in a dream, you move around through the crowd receiving congratulations. You drink in the rewards; you revel in the glory of success.
>
> What you love most about the whole thing is _____ .
> What you can hardly wait to have now is _____ .
> What makes it all worthwhile is _____ .

As you replay this scene in your mind, allow the full-blown feelings and sensations of the event to emerge, and see what motivates you. When you are ready, begin to write a list of "What Motivates Me Most."

Here's another scenario for you to imagine:

> You are strolling along a secluded riverbank. The weather is perfect: a huge azure sky with cotton-pillow clouds hovers over the green meadow on the opposite bank. Blossoming dogwood and weeping

willow trees bend over the clear, lightly rippled water. "This is the life," you muse. "Everything I've ever wanted to experience is mine now.

I have _____.

I love _____.

_____ feels so good!"

✧◆✧

Again, allow the pleasurable and enjoyable feelings of this scene to remind you of rewards that are motivating for you. Recall the experience of feelings that you prize, sensations you would travel to the ends of the Earth to claim as your own. Write about your insights in your Dream Journal and workbook.

Too many people, if pressed, would have to admit that *pain* is one of their primary motivators. We sit on a hornet's nest until it becomes too uncomfortable to stay there anymore. When the dysfunction in our relationship becomes intolerable, when the clutter, sickness, disintegration, or dishonesty we are embroiled in becomes unbearable, we are finally pushed to our limit, and only then do we act to bring about a change.

I asked one young man who had taken my workshop how his dream was progressing. He responded, "Let's face it, I'm a hopeless procrastinator." "So, is that what you want your tombstone to say?" I asked in reply. If so, then he was moving in the direction he wanted to go. If not, then what was he going to do about it?

Eleanor is a woman who came to me for some private coaching, frustrated after having spent three years undergoing professional counseling without significant improvement in her condition. She told me that all she learned was that she was depressed. She had picked up a label to pin on her symptoms, and she had even come to understand some of the dynamics of her depression, but she continued to *be* depressed.

"But," I asked, "is this what you want?" "No, of course not," she replied with some surprise. "Then let's identify what it is that depresses you, and what your options are in those areas. Let's also identify the times when you are *not* feeling depressed and find out what you can do to create more of *those* times for yourself, right now."

Eleanor disclosed that her depression originated when her mother began living with her. The most obvious option (finding another place for her mother to live), seemed impossible to her, which was why she felt blocked. I asked her, "Is there a way for your mother to remain with you without your continuing to be depressed about it?" We began to explore the types of adjustments and communications that would help clear up problems in the arrangement. Was she willing to make the changes necessary to eliminate the causes of her depression? That was still an important question. But in the meantime, I encouraged her to do more of the activities that made her feel good.

"You don't have to wait until all your problems are solved before you begin building the healthy self you want to develop," I said. "Why don't you decide to start taking some definite action to bring increased happiness into your life right now? People sometimes don't realize that you *can* do both simultaneously."

It is a principle of metaphysics that whatever you put your energy into will increase in your experience. Perhaps you have had an injury that hurt so much you could hardly stand it. Then someone distracted you or your interest was caught up by something outside yourself. Later, you became aware that you had spent quite some time without ever giving a single thought to your pain. But the minute you went back to it, the pain grew progressively worse and worse. In this way, pain can be the motivator that draws our attention to what we *don't* want. But rather than focusing on the pain and fostering its escalation, why not start right now to focus on what we *do* want? We do have the option of allowing positive, satisfying rewards to be the motivators we choose.

As parents, we often interject motivating influences into our child-rearing strategies. "You can't go outside to play until your room is cleaned up," we say. "If you sit very quietly in church, we'll go to the park afterwards." We may design a chart and put stars up on it to reinforce desired behaviors. When we become adults, it's up to us to become nurturing parents to ourselves. We must make sure there are plenty of gold stars to reward the behaviors we want to encourage in ourselves.

"What do you like to do when you're feeling good, not depressed?" I asked Eleanor. She replied, "When I'm going for a bike ride out in the sunshine—that always lifts my spirits. Or when I go to a really good play." "And when did you last do those things?" was my next question. "Six years ago," she said.

Eleanor's example is instructive because we all have a tendency to forget to build the reinforcing rewards that help us feel good into our daily life. Once Eleanor built some rewards into her life, her attitude and perspective changed, and her depression lifted. Life is now a joyful journey for her.

So ask the following questions yourself now: What kind of rewards or reinforcers motivate you? What "carrot" will keep you running tirelessly around the track? Do you work for the money? For the chance to play? For the sheer joy of personal achievement? For applause and recognition? My strongest motivator is the joy of being able to go to sleep knowing I've done the very best I could today, and will tomorrow, too. Make a list in your Dream Journal and workbook of your personal positive motivators.

Wendy was a highly successful executive in a multinational sales firm. She was midway through the "Live Your Dream" workshop when she received a promotion to a top-level position in Japan. Identifying her motivators was essential to Wendy's gathering the inner strength this new position would require of her. She could not afford to allow her energy to be scattered, and she must know where to plug in to get her batteries recharged. She probed deep within, until she came to an inner assurance about her source of motivation. Here's what she learned: "It's not about money, for me. It's not about prestige or titles. Now, I'll finally have the position where I can give my all as a successful businesswoman. It's me being in love with myself."

My friend the "procrastinator" decided that he was motivated by a sense of accomplishment. He realized that scheduling the hours of his day and making a list of everything he accomplished that day would motivate him to stop procrastinating and get to work. The next time I visited his office; I noted that one whole wall was covered with several weeks' worth of lists showing what he had accomplished each day. Every time he looked up, he felt rewarded and motivated anew. I didn't have to ask what he was doing to realize his dream; it was written all over the wall. "Let's face it, I'm too busy living my dream and becoming world-famous to have any time for procrastination," he joked.

Build More Motivators Into Your Life

There are many other techniques for motivating yourself. You may say to yourself, "I will not leave the office until everything is cleared off this desk tonight" or "just twenty more pages, then I can take a coffee break." One of the most effective methods is to ask someone to support you living your dream. Ask your dream partner to call you and offer frequent encouragement and reminders. I know of a real-estate salesman who promised to take his family camping every time he made a sale; his children became enthusiastic supporters of his success at work.

Following are some other ways people in my workshops have chosen to build more motivators into their everyday lives:

- ✦ Exercise daily.

- ✦ Put up notes around the house to remind myself to put first things (my dream) first.

- ✦ Treat myself to more walks on the beach.

- ✦ Set aside time each day just for myself.

- ✦ Play motivational tapes while I'm driving.

- ✦ Meditate daily.

- ✦ Buy myself flowers.

- ✦ Plan mini-vacations to reward small milestones.

Fulfilled and successful people do not spend a lot of time sitting around waiting for the phone to ring, for someone else to come and pump them up, or for the needed inspiration to carry on. Neither do they pretend they require no motivators and no support. They take charge, in this area as in others, of anticipating and providing for their own needs. Building motivators into your life is a powerful way to assure that your dream will receive the ongoing nourishment it needs, especially when the going gets tough or you are under pressure or stress. So go back into your Dream Journal and workbook now, and write your personal plan for making those rewards that motivate you a part of the realization of your dream.

PINPOINT YOUR NATURAL GIFTS AND TALENTS

So far in this in-depth personal inventory, you have been challenged to identify what values you esteem and what your motivators are. As you work in these areas, you will find yourself moving closer and closer to knowing for sure who you truly are. You will begin living in harmony with the real inside *you*. Once you find it, you will want to express the real you more fully and more joyously in the world.

As you become more inner-directed, you may find yourself rejecting many of the old ways of expressing yourself that were based on your former, limited understanding of who you are. Best-selling author Dr. Wayne Dyer says, "Would you pay a 14-year-old or a 17-year-old for advice on how to live the rest of your life? Yet most of us live our lives out of decisions we made when we were fourteen or seventeen." As you look afresh at many of your life decisions, you may want to choose new ways of being that are more congruent with yourself today.

You can only be fully self-expressive when you know what your natural gifts and talents are. Identifying which talents come naturally to you is the third ingredient in consolidating a congruent you.

Have you ever admired movie stars or great musicians for the sheer naturalness of their performance? Have you envied an entertainer or teacher whose work seemed more like play because he or she loved it so much? The link you felt with that person was a connection with your desire to have that much joy doing whatever comes naturally to you.

On the other hand, picture those frustrated individuals who bend every ounce of willpower to climb to the top of a field in which they have little natural talent or the miserable person who tries against all odds to force the wrong relationship to work.

During my teaching years, I kept a sign on my office wall that read "We Are All Gifted." It was a highly controversial message in a public school setting, because of its implied challenge for us as teachers: *to find and enhance the gift* in each and every child.

I have had so many adults—35, 45, 60 years old—come into my workshops still vaguely troubled by the questions "what am I going to be when I grow up?" and "what do I want to do with my life?" And I've had so many who finally realized that where they've worked so hard to get is not where they want to be at all. Then they say, "Oh, no! Do I really want to go ahead with this?" as the mounting discomfort surfaces.

So be forewarned: You may come to a stunning realization that makes you want to run back home and hide in your closet. You may be tempted to crawl back into that smaller shell of yourself where you were comfortable and secure. But if you're not living from your true self—that greater being you now know you are—you won't be living your dream.

Acknowledge Yourself

The third part of this in-depth personal inventory can help you identify your natural gifts and talents. Begin by examining some activity you recently completed and listing everything you can possibly think of about it to acknowledge yourself for. Acknowledge yourself for all the little things involved. For example: I got home on time (I am usually punctual—good for me!), and I took care to water all the way to the corners of the yard (I did a thorough job. I am a conscientious person who takes pride in my work). I worked quickly and efficiently, pulling out the dandelions at the same time. I interrupted the job to give my child my total attention for a few minutes (I honor my child's needs and take good care of him); then I went right back to finish the job (My ability to carry through a task to completion has grown immensely!). I respected my body and peace of mind enough to sit down and relax for 10 minutes, so I'll be able to handle the demands of my family with renewed energy.

This exercise—acknowledging yourself in writing—is an effective tool in building self-esteem. Use it whenever you have a need to feel better about yourself. Try using it in situations where you feel terrible about how you've been doing, writing about all the good you can extract from your experience. Once again, you will demonstrate the magic of focusing your attention on the positive. You will experience great benefits from tending to and nurturing your self-esteem; why hang around waiting for someone else to pay you a compliment and make you feel good? This exercise also helps to identify the individual components of your natural talents and gifts—breaking down broad skills and abilities into specific elements.

When you use your most natural curiosities, strengths and talents, you can grow and express yourself powerfully and effortlessly. In contrast, if you are trying to force yourself to become good at something that goes against your grain, you are likely to struggle every inch of the way. You may be able to succeed—but how much more successful might you be at something that comes naturally to you? Discovering exactly what your natural gifts are—and are not—is crucial to maximizing your potential.

Identify What Comes Naturally

What do you bring into the world that is uniquely you, that is yours alone to give, that is your mission? Let's return to take a closer look at who you were as a very young child, as well as who you are now. In your Dream Journal and workbook, write quick answers to these questions, applying them to the earliest age you can remember:

✦ What did you like to do most as a young child? Did you build bridges or block towers? (A cousin of mine used to play at building bridges and "traveling" all over. He grew up to become a state highway engineer responsible for designing beautiful transportation systems and bridges.) Were you the entertainer? Did you put on plays or performances? Did you direct them? Did you feel most alive when you were playing a role? Were you the farmer? Planner? Organizer? Teacher? Peace-maker?

✦ What words did you use to ask questions? Did you want to know *why* or *how?* Were you curious about how things worked, or were you more interested in explaining the mysteries of life or in finding out what made up the tiny parts of a flower or weed? Did you want to understand people, or nature, or intellectual concepts, or mechanical objects? What truths were you already intuitively certain about, even as a child?

✦ What were you good at? At home? In school?

✦ What are you good at now? Are you a detail person, a trouble-shooter, or an administrator? Are you exceptionally good at getting along with people? Can you bring out the best in others or make them feel at ease and appreciated? Are you skilled at enrolling others in projects you initiate? Do you run a tight ship or give great parties? List 20 things you do very well. Break each activity down to identify within it what the separate components are that you particularly enjoy. (Note: This list will be most beneficial if you summarize and record it in your workbook and continue to add to it and modify it on an ongoing basis.)

✦ What makes you feel most alive? List five experiences you've had recently when you felt vitally alive. Beside each, identify *what* it was about the experience that made you feel so good.

✦ When do you feel most highly energized? List five activities that give you so much energy that nothing else matters when you're doing them. You forget about time, and about being tired or hungry or bored or lonely, you become so engrossed.

✦ What experiences have you had recently where you felt absolute joy? Write *how* you brought this about.

When do you feel the happiest? As a natural teacher, I feel my greatest joy when someone, out of my guidance, is growing and becoming more of who they are.

Anna, one of my workshop participants, listed cooking as one of her skills. Breaking down the experience of cooking into more specific details, Anna wrote:

"I love to create new dishes and modify recipes I find, to improve them and make them unusual. I love to invent stimulating mixes of new flavors, colors, and textures—the *artistry* of food preparation. I enjoy being the agent of transformation, as raw materials are turned into exquisite culinary creations. I enjoy testing myself at handling routine procedures simultaneously and efficiently—the organizational aspect of it. I love the compliments I get about how wonderful my cooking is. I feel a sort of detached amazement that 'I did this!' followed by a self-affirming, 'But of course—I am good!' And I love to taste my creations myself. I even enjoy the satisfaction of seeing all the pots and pans and mess cleaned up and put away afterwards. And I like giving people the feeling of being specially cared for."

When Anna looked back over her writing, she realized how important being an artist and a creator were to her. She also knew her gifts were stimulated and rewarded most in a social context and she would not be happy as, say, an isolated studio artist. She noted that managing events and the details of a production was an experience she relished. Integrating these conclusions with those she drew from writing about other activities helped Anna develop a clearer picture of herself.

Another woman I know discovered her ideal career by a process of exploration similar to Anna's. Barbara came up with several specific characteristics she would want to express in the perfect job. It would be one where her critical mind would be an asset, and one in which she could bring her varied experience together, keep learning, read a lot, be creative, and decide independently how to spend her time. When she had listed all this, Barbara could not imagine such a job. She set her list aside and went on as usual with her job search. But within two years, she found herself in an editing position that miraculously combined all these different aspects.

If you are seeking greater career satisfaction, take some time now to prepare a similar list of your ideal requirements. From your answers to the questions posed previously, write the characteristics your ideal career position will have. Be sure to mention ways in which your natural talents and skills will be used.

Another way to identify your natural gifts is to take a survey of 15 people who know you. Ask them questions such as, "What am I good at?" and "What do you think my talents and skills are?" As you receive their responses, write them down. Take some time to consider the feedback you receive, appreciating that *you* are still the world's foremost authority on yourself and that you will be the ultimate judge of its validity. Ask yourself, *Is that true for me? Does this person see something I overlooked?*

PUT YOUR VALUES, MOTIVATORS, AND TALENTS TO WORK FOR YOU

Having inventoried your values, motivators, and talents, you are now ready to take charge and put this information to use. The next step is to develop a plan for accomplishing your dreams.

Develop Your Dream Plan

Begin by setting aside eight pages in your Dream Journal and writing one of the following titles on each page:

◆ Physical Body.

◆ Relationships.

◆ Career.

◆ Work and Home Environment.

◆ Mental State of Being.

◆ Spiritual Life.

◆ Financial Well-Being.

◆ Leisure/Recreation.

Now, on each page, down the left-hand side, write these headings:

My Ideal Self in:

◆ My Entire Lifetime.

◆ 10 Years.

◆ 5 Years.

◆ 1 Year.

◆ 6 Months.

◆ 3 Months.

Whenever someone calls me a "dreamer," I smile, because I know it is true. I also know that the other side of dreaming the dream is that I am willing to do the work needed to bring the dream into reality. This is the point where many people get stuck. The dream must be translated into quantifiable stages and manageable tasks, which must be accomplished one step at a time. It may take time and hard work, and it is unlikely to come about by magic or fervent wishfulness.

Magic will sometimes happen, but a step-by-step plan may be needed as well.

If your dream is to get a college degree, the steps you must take are laid out for you in advance. You will take the required classes the first year, do all the homework and term papers, and pass the exams. You will be thinking about choosing a major area of interest. Advisors are there to guide you along the way and answer your questions.

But what if another part of your dream is to have ever-present peace of mind? What classes can you take? If there is no established program, you may have to design one of your own. This may involve experimenting to find ways that will work for you. It may mean false starts and regrouping for a renewed drive. Your game tactics and strategies will need to be reviewed and updated often, as new information comes in and new directions are chosen.

I am always excited whenever someone discovers, "Well, my dream is not what I thought it was." This says to me that they are moving deeper and deeper into themselves. Often, the way we zero in on our dream is to state what we believe our dream to be right now, start working on it, and learn as we get there that "that's not it, but now I'm closer to knowing what it *is*."

Knowing that it's never possible to produce a final, set-in-concrete plan, we must start where we are right now to develop a flexible, working model for accomplishing each part of our dream. As they are in most human enterprises, the thinking and planning stages are vital to successfully realizing the result. Consider carefully: Are you willing to do this work? If not, when will you be? What will happen if you put it off until later?

When you are ready to take your commitment to your dream onward, turn to the first of the eight Dream Plan pages that you have prepared (the one titled Physical Body). Look back at your Dream Boards and the other work you have completed so far, and make a list of the aspects of your dream that relate to your physical body. You might want to include your ideal health, weight, appearance, and exercise program. For each item, decide what actions and results you intend to accomplish within a 10-year, five-year, one-year, six-month, and three-month time period. Note specific dates so you can refer back to them and gauge how well you're meeting your projected schedule. Your first page might look something like the sample on page 112.

My Dream Self: Physical Body   Today's Date: _____

TIME	WEIGHT	RESULT	ACTION
Lifetime	125 lb.	Radiant health.	Exercise or walk daily.
10 Years	125 lb.	Free of allergies.	Reach goal of climbing Mt. Kilamanjaro.
5 years	125 lb.	Sneezing and difficulty in breathing in the past; breathing free and clear all the time.	Hike Mts. Shasta and Rainier.
1 Year	125 lb.	Install air-filtering system.	Train for mountain climbing.
6 Months	150 lb.	Decrease red meat to twice a week; continue allergy treatment regimen.	Join athletic club and start mountain climbing classes.
3 Months	165 lb. 160 lb. 155 lb.	Make an appointment with allergist; vacuum for dust twice weekly.	Aerobic dance class three times a week.

On pages 113 and 114 are two sample pages one dreamer developed as a plan for realizing the mental and spiritual needs of a dream.

My Dream Self: Mental State of Being

Time	Result	Action
Lifetime	To have expanded my creative intuitive and logical powers to maximum capacity. To acquire a vast familiarity with the accumulated knowledge and culture of the ages, and to develop the wisdom and understanding of a sage.	Read from great books of the world daily. Attend cultural events twice a month. Cultivate friendships with wise people from all over the world and continue in my journaling to see inner guidance in making wise life decisions.
10 Years	Gain expertise in various world cultures through study, classes, and cultural involvement, being a learner as well as a teacher.	Guide anthropological expedition to Zaire; visit the foreign minister and bestow museum endowment for preservation of Zairian artifacts and culture.
	Identify principles of "Live Your Dream" found in other cultural heritages; discover myths and folk tales teaching these principles.	Teach "Live Your Dream" in many countries, adapting it skillfully to incorporate appropriate cultural variations.
5 Years	Have greatly expanded horizons and contacts. Increase my information continually, and become a meaningful contributor.	Travel to Switzerland and Italy. Cultivate friends who are experts in many fields. Select an organization and become a substantial contributing member. Purchase the Great Book series and encyclopedia; read daily.
1 Year	Increase my formal and informal education.	Subscribe to mini-lecture series at the university; acquire collection of music tapes and art reprints representative of many cultures; take music appreciation and art history classes.
6 Months	Attend six cultural events and read five books. Become informed about world travel and begin planning first trip.	Start a book review group meeting twice monthly. Research travel arrangements and contact travel agent.
3 Months	Select an area that I know nothing about, and write a list of books I want to read to become knowledgeable in that area.	Take a travel preparatory class on Europe.

My Dream Self: Spiritual Life

Time	Result	Action
Lifetime	Turn over all decisions to a Higher Power. Be living my life at the total state of acceptance. Become a transcended master. Be prepared to celebrate the death cycle as part of the life cycle and to meet my Maker in peace.	Be a master practicing.
10 Years	Establish such a strong connection with my Source that others are empowered. Be a channel of divine empowerment.	Go public with my message (television and radio worldwide).
5 Years	Demonstrate that I am empowered by an unlimited Source.	Give talks; facilitate workshops sourced by Higher Power.
1 Year	Experience joy at will. Passion for life is my motivating force.	Meditate daily, opening myself to more and greater joy, love, and inspiration.
6 Months	Turn everything over to a Higher Power—of free choice, not just in desperation. Get myself out of the way. Write what I will do based on my daily log.	Keep a record of my successes each time I turn something over. Take actions indicated by my writing.
3 Months	Develop awareness of what my fears are of trusting in a Higher Power, and of the choices I make (to trust or panic).	Keep a daily log of my trusting and doubting thoughts. Record the amounts of time I spend on creative, trusting solutions vs. time spent doubting. Read inspirational books and listen to tapes daily.

Visualize End Results

Continue completing your remaining Dream Plan pages in this same way. When you have finished, you may wish to combine the information you have compiled and display it in a vivid visual way. One of my strategies has been to, after identifying clearly what I want to accomplish, imagine seeing my result (my ultimate dream) in the highest corner of every room I walk into.

Try creating a personal graphic design that will represent your Dream Plan at a glance. You might develop a flow chart, cluster drawing, tree, or yellow brick road—or think of a different design, uniquely your own! Let your imagination go, release your creativity, and really have fun with this.

Keep It Current

The very fact that you have now stated your Dream Plan and identified its working stages has set in motion the process of realizing your dream. As you continue to do the work necessary to keep to your schedule, review what you have written in your Dream Journal and workbook and look at your Dream Plan periodically. You may decide to change parts of your dream or of the stages and steps you have plotted along its course. You will undoubtedly be astonished at the progress you have made if you truly commit yourself to each aspect of your dream.

And watch out: Your life may change! You will uncover possibilities and potential you never knew you had. You will discover all you were meant to be. You will *become* your dream.

Dreamwork Checklist

❑ Commit to at least 15 minutes daily visualizing yourself living your dream, and write your thoughts in your Dream Journal.

❑ Keep reading your affirmations, morning and night.

❑ Make a list of the steps you've taken so far toward realizing your dream. List completed items, steps accomplished in them, successes, and milestones.

❑ Live according to your values. Pay attention to whether you are doing this or not.

❑ Build inner-directed motivators into your everyday life.

❑ Acknowledge yourself often, and deliberately build your self-esteem. Acknowledge others, too.

❑ Think about and list activities that bring you joy and aliveness.

❑ Work with your dream partner to repeatedly drill each other on the question, "What are you best at?" Give quick, spontaneous responses—whatever pops into your mind.

❑ Add one item every day to your list of natural gifts and talents.

❑ Outline the specifications of your ideal dream job.

❑ Create your Dream Plan and begin work on it.

❑ Create an imaginative visual display that shows the steps and stages of your Dream Plan.

❑ Call your dream partner five times a week and ask how you can assist him or her in living according to his or her values. Share what motivators are influencing you right now, and ask about your partner's Dream Plan progress.

ASK JOYCE!

Q: After reading Chapter 4, I began to realize I was not living true to my values. I was telling my friends I wanted to write, but I never wrote. I realize now that I have to change either my dream or change myself to make my dream come true. Is there hope for me or will I be a procrastinator forever?

A: In Dorothy Gilman's book, *A New Kind of Country,* she states the importance of "living with eyes wide open." It may help you to live more congruently if you plan your daily schedule to include what you say you want (to write) and then commit to living with your eyes wide open as you observe yourself. The hardest part may be telling yourself the truth. You may not be willing to commit to your dream.

   I do know the joy of living true to yourself is worth the effort. And this is ultimately your decision.

Q: To "look for the learning," as you suggest, is a very new way of thinking. How do you suggest I do this without becoming obsessive?

A: The easiest new habit to "look at the learning" is to reread what you write in your Dream Journal and workbook. Simply ask yourself questions such as these:

   ❖ *What have I learned by living this experience?*

   ❖ *Is this a new concept for me?*

   ❖ *What will I do to make new choices that support and empower me to live my dream?*

   ❖ *Is it time to take action or make a "to do in the future" list?*

   I am not an advocate of letting go of "something" if you find yourself annoyed or even paying attention to it. If a life experience "has" your attention, my guess is that there is a learning experience present. Don't miss it!

Q: Asking myself, *What motivates me?* is definitely something I have never done. I am having a difficult time identifying what I am motivated by. I can't seem to fill in the blanks in the workbook. What do I do?

A: As you now realize, the *Live Your Dream* book series was designed to invite you, the reader, to delve into who you are and who you want to be. The subtitle of the workbook reads "Discover and Live the Life of Your Dreams."

   There is no easy or quick way to arrive at truly knowing yourself. I advise you get out your pen and think of it as a shovel or pick that you will use to find the treasure that is within you.

Q: I asked 15 people what they thought my natural gifts were. This has been, surprisingly, a nurturing exercise. My question to you is: What if they saw things I do not see? Should I just accept it or try to live up to their opinion of me? Should I consider these as new opportunities to explore even though I know in my heart I have absolutely no desire to discern if I have any talents in those areas? I am afraid I may miss my true calling.

A: You may indeed have the talent to be a world-class painter, but if the desire is not there all that talent will not make you happy. Although others may see gifts in us, it is never a sure bet that those are avenues that we will want to explore. What your friends are seeing are the many facets that make up the composition that is you. One lifetime cannot possibly give you enough time to study each facet. You, ultimately, must decide where to put your energies. Do it wholeheartedly and without regret.

Q: I finished doing all the assignments and now have my Dream Plan. It looks great on paper, but I can't seem to put it in action. Will you please give some ideas to inspire me to get busy?

A: You are not alone! Here are some coaching tips to consider:
   - Hire an "expert" when you know what you need and are ready for guidance and advice.
   - Join a group, club, or organization for support and empowerment.
   - Ask you dream partner to hold you accountable.
   - Make sure your daily schedule includes activities and tasks that are congruent with your dream.

Q: I still seem to have more questions than answers. Will you give me some tips to follow so that I don't waste my time distracting myself?

A: Certainly. Here you go:
   - Make a list of your questions to ask someone who has a dream similar to yours.
   - Arrange to meet with a Dream Coach or a mentor to share the list of questions you wrote.
   - Take an action step you are advised to take and reward yourself in some way when you follow through.
   - Make a lasting change that will bring you new energy.
   - Copy this quote by Jean Bolen into your list of questions as a reminder to reach out for answers and inspiration: "When a question is well framed, the answer will come."

*Your Power to Turn
Negatives Into Positives*

*There is no such thing as a problem without a gift for you in
its hands. You seek problems because you need their gifts.*

—Richard Bach, *Illusions*

Problems or challenges appear in our lives from time to time. There are
days when everything seems to be going wrong, and we proclaim with exas-
peration, "You'll never prove to *me* that any good is coming out of this!"
Yet we can look so objectively at the lives of others and see that it's not the
problem that can make or break you; it is *what you make* of it.

Do you make mountains out of molehills, or do you make molehills out
of mountains? Do you look at your difficulties with appreciation or regret?
In this chapter, you will have an opportunity to practice techniques that
can enable you to make the most of every situation you're involved in. Turning a handicap into a victory is the stuff from which heroes are made. You've
seen the movies, read the books, dreamed some of the same dreams—and
you can do it, too, from one moment to the next, starting now.

Challenges often do turn into growth experiences. Charlene, a woman
who had been married for 14 years, was faced with the shock of her
husband's leaving her suddenly for another woman. Never having worked
seriously to earn a living and now responsible for the support of three re-
bellious teenagers and an expensive home, Charlene did not view this as a
positive opportunity in her life—at first. But within six months, she had
identified a career goal and found a job that would sustain her while she
took night classes to get a degree. She had even enlisted the aid of her
children and developed her family into a cooperative unit, all helping out
through this difficult time.

Charlene began to be deeply appreciative and excited about the new
life that was opening up to her. Suddenly she recognized how stifled and

bored she had been before and how reluctant to make changes in her too-comfortable life. What had seemed a tragedy evolved into a new, much more fulfilling life for Charlene.

LOOK BEYOND THE STRUGGLE

Is it time for you to stop suffering and struggling, to relax and peacefully accept a change, and to turn your energy into making your problem situation into a learning experience? In your Dream Journal, write answers to the following questions:

✦ What useful purpose do my suffering and resistance to change serve?

✦ Do I need this purpose to grow stronger in some way?

✦ Do I learn *more,* the harder I struggle and suffer?

Someone once said, "What is our pain but the breaking of the shell that encloses our understanding?" We can try to clutch at the pieces of the shell as it crumbles around us, or we can leap out and go exploring in a new world.

Vicki Noble, author of *Motherpeace,* captured this idea beautifully when she wrote, "The destruction of the old always precedes the building of the new, but one can choose which side to be on." Which side do you want to choose? If you feel like you're being dragged along, kicking and screaming in the currents of change, looking for the gift in the situation may be the last thing in the world you want to do. Or is it? Once you begin to reach toward the light at the end of the tunnel, your attachment to the swirling confusion around you loosens. And the faster you can change your focus, the less you will ever feel yourself at the mercy of life's events.

A kite rises against, not with, the wind. Opposition is often what teaches us. Conflict wakes us up. Have you ever noticed with surprise that you had actually *chosen* a problem as a way of motivating yourself?

Andrew encouraged his wife, "Go ahead. Take that acting class in New York if that's what you want to do." The moment she was gone, however, he found himself engulfed in doubt and paralyzing loneliness. He knew that *she* was growing and changing. Things could not go on any longer as they had been.

Without his wife, he realized it was up to him to get himself motivated. Finally, staring into the mirror, he came to a powerful conclusion: "*I* don't like *myself* like this—how could anyone else like me? I've got to make some changes. It's either grow or die!"

Andrew had begun his week feeling lonely, deserted, helpless, and clinging. He and his wife had avoided being apart with fervor unmatched in many of their other endeavors. To his credit, Andrew was able to use this opportunity to break out of his pattern of dependency. He ended the week having faced the truth about himself for the first time in years. He was ready to make some changes.

Another person who was jarred by a problem into making some unanticipated changes is Alice. She lived in a beautiful large condominium in an expensive area of town. But her lifestyle was really more luxurious than she could afford. As the bills began mounting up and she was forced to evaluate her finances, she realized she could not pay such high rent. She went through an agonizing struggle. Where would she go? What could she do? Would she be able to find a place she liked? She recalled:

> "I had to move, and when I didn't find a place by the end of the month, I made a decision that freed me, temporarily, from all the doubts and questions. I put all my possessions into storage, packed my three kids and dog into the car, and drove to the Midwest, where I had once lived. There we were able to stay with friends and I could continue my consulting work until I could save enough money to come back home.
>
> "The comfort of being with friends who cared, and getting away from it all, gave me the freedom I needed to think things over. *Exactly what do I want?* I kept asking myself. Once I knew that, I could make a plan for getting it. Before long, we were able to return home and rent a small apartment in a very low-budget section of town. There we put up with midnight brawls in the street just outside our window, and every day I drove the kids all the way to the other side of the city so they could attend their old school—until, finally, I saved enough to move back to the area we loved.
>
> "Out of this adventure, I was able to find a small, modest but wonderful house that is perfect for us, right in my old neighborhood! I had been content before in the big condo, and I might never have thought of moving. But now I am happier than ever in my new, perfect little house—and the whole experience has been invaluable in teaching me to be clear about what I really want—and to live within my means."

Take a Third-Party View

I often encourage clients to write about a problem as if it were someone else's story. This has proven to be a valuable technique for turning negatives into positives. After you've completed "your story," read it over several times. With the detachment of an uninvolved third party, you may be able to see your situation from a new perspective. Ask yourself, *What am I learning from this problem? What advice might I give to someone else facing these circumstances?* Write several feedback sentences for yourself.

Go into your Dream Journal and workbook now, and take some time to write about three problem situations presently going on in your life. As soon as you finish, call your dream partner or a dreamer friend and share your insights.

The third-person view is also a valuable technique to use when you decide it's time to understand unresolved issues you experienced as a child. Try testing the exercise now. Recall several childhood memories and write each as "someone else's story." Work with a memory that seems to block you from realizing a dream you have. As you write, keep in mind that the goal of this exercise is to turn what seemed to be a negative into a positive. Like an author who already has planned a story's plot, mold your story to reach the conclusion of what a *gift* that "problem" was!

There is always a gift in the problem situation. We turn our problems into opportunities when we allow ourselves to stop struggling, let down our resistance, and graciously accept the gift.

Gwen's ego felt defeated when she lost the election to the state senate seat—a goal she had given up a dedicated legal career to pursue. The campaign had been a hard and bitter one, and her opponent's smear tactics had churned up rough water for her to tread. Months later, she looked back on the outcome with gratitude. Working as a political science professor was much better suited to her nature, she now saw clearly. And her election experiences had broadened her knowledge of the field immeasurably. Every member of her class had also passed through an in-depth exploration of ethical campaign practices.

THE POWER OF YOUR DREAM TO WEATHER THE STORM

As you move toward becoming your dream, you will unavoidably find that everything in your life that is *not* like your dream will come up for you to handle. We often create some "rain" to give ourselves a little time to get ready for the changes we must face. We clear away the storm by riveting our eyes firmly on the rainbow of our dream and moving steadfastly through the clouds.

I used to visit my grandchildren in a seaport village where it was foggy and rainy most of the time. Every time I planned a visit, I would tell the children, "I love warm, sunny days. So let's know that we'll have a sunny day when I come." They would hold the thought, "The sun is shining for the good of all concerned. And *we want that now.*" And when I arrived, the weather was miraculously beautiful. One day little Cathy told her preschool class, "My grandma *is* the sun!"

I have found Cathy's belief in me and in herself to be very empowering. The truth is that *we all are the sun*—when we move right through the clouds and rain to the clear skies beyond.

The way out of the rain clouds is to start asking questions. *If* I create the storm, what purpose is it serving for me now? What can I learn? What is to be gained from the difficulty I must face? What do I need to do to clear away the storm and bring out the sun?

Joseph, a workshop participant, followed his dream through a tempestuous storm to the clearing beyond. In his early 30s, he discovered that he had always wanted to move far out into the country and farm his own land. When Joseph decided at last to make this major change in his life, he began at once to look for suitable properties. His hopes were soon dashed by the discovery that he was already too far in debt to qualify for the essential loan. *I just can't do it,* he thought. *It's too late. There's no way.* The storm moved in.

But one sunny morning he remembered that he knew how to make good use of his problems. He began asking the questions necessary to discover the learning in the dilemma he faced. Soon the realization dawned about what he would have to learn and do: In order to be able to trust himself with owning his own farm, he had to build up credibility with himself that he could be financially responsible. He had to learn to keep tight control of his spending and to channel his resources into his most important purposes.

It might take a few years of concentrated effort, but he would use the time to work hard and pay off all his past debts. In the meantime, he could take agricultural extension classes, learn the business aspects of farm management and prepare himself in many ways to embark successfully on his new life. When he was finally able to buy his farm, Joseph made the move much better equipped to succeed than if he had done so impulsively three years earlier.

FINDING THE ELUSIVE GIFT

The gift in the problem situation is sometimes obvious, other times not. The athlete who sprains an ankle misses the championship competition and is thus spared the agony of defeat or the challenges success might bring; the person whose arrest for drunk driving channels him into a rehabilitation program; the flat tire on the way to a meeting you hated having to attend; failing a qualifying exam for a field that is stifling—often, such experiences give us clarity about what we really want.

Our resistance to receiving the gift usually comes from clinging to a different result. The gift only becomes available once we let go, release our expectations that things *should* be different, and open ourselves to the learning.

A Formula for Release

Here's another technique to release yourself from being stuck in a problem and to help you find its gift instead. Use the following list of questions. Either ask your dream partner to read them to you and tape record the answers, or work on your own, writing the answers in your Dream Journal and workbook. You may find this method valuable for many issues now and in the future.

✦ What is bothering me?

✦ What are the effects of this issue on me—mentally, physically, and emotionally?

✦ What is the effect of the issue on those around me?

✦ What does the issue cause me to do or not do?

✦ What are the advantages of these effects, with respect to living my dream?

✦ What are the disadvantages of these effects, with respect to living my dream?

✦ How would life be different if the issue were gone?

✦ Why do I need the issue?

✦ What beliefs do I have that explain how this issue might have developed?

✦ What are the payoffs for keeping the status quo regarding this issue?

One dreamer gave the following answers to these questions. Note how his discoveries unfolded.

✦ *What is bothering me?* Most of all, it's the fear that I won't have enough money to pay my bills as the first of the month rolls around.

✦ *What are the effects of this issue on me?* Well, mentally, it has me worrying a lot. I go over and over in my mind, what I could do if this or that happened? What else could I possibly give up or do without, if I have to? What's the worst scenario? My attention seems riveted to the problems. Emotionally and spiritually, I withdraw into my fears and myself. I'm not able to do the creative work I need to do, and this aggravates the problem further, because when I'm more productive, I make more money.

◆ *What are the effects of this issue on others?* As I isolate myself, my children feel abandoned and worried, also. Their behavior gets worse, making my life even more difficult. Friends I could turn to for help or understanding see me as distant and aloof, so they leave me alone.

◆ *What does the issue cause me to do or not do?* Because of my preoccupied fear, I become very cautious about taking any risks. I get into the survival mode, leaving the creative mode behind. I make calculated judgments based on minimizing my losses— rather than saying what I want and just going after it. I don't go to professional seminars or seek out coaching that would help me to advance in my career. My holding back extends to my social life and leisure time as well. I don't laugh, or dance, or play, or go outside and enjoy myself as much. I feel afraid and tense.

◆ *What are the advantages of these effects, with respect to living my dream?* Well, I suppose I could think of a few. For one thing, I am more careful not to waste money. I am forced to choose what's most important to spend my money on and eliminate the less important activities and purchases. That keeps me focused, with less scattering of attention and resources. I know I can't afford not to get my work done, so I push myself harder. I take my responsibilities more seriously, and I am more independent.

◆ *What are the disadvantages of these effects, with respect to living my dream?* I feel burdened, not free. My energy is constricted. I am troubled that I'm not being the role model I want my kids to have. I'm stewing in lack and limitation as I'm telling my daughter to pull out all the stops, go to college, and become a doctor. Most of all, I tend to forget about my *dream* altogether, I'm so caught up in dealing with one problem after another!

◆ *How would life be different if the issue were gone?* Simple! I'd go out and do all the things I want to do, stop worrying, and get out there and live my dream! (Of course, I don't know if I'd be *as* productive, or push myself quite so hard. Maybe I'd be lazy, if I didn't *have* to worry so much about the money.)

◆ *Why do I need the issue?* Now that's a hard one. Let me think…. Maybe I have to prove to myself that I can be trusted. And that I can handle it all—I am strong. I weathered the storm. Maybe even a little self-righteousness: One day I'll look at all the people who underestimated me and say, "I told you so!" Also, as I said before, it helps keep me motivated and moving. On the other hand, maybe I *don't* actually *need* this issue at all! Maybe I could accomplish what I want without it, now that I see what my choices are!

◆ *What beliefs do I have that explain how this issue might have developed?* Several come to mind:

  ✧ You have to work *hard* for what you get.

  ✧ You can't have it all—you have to choose.

  ✧ There's barely enough to go around.

  ✧ Why would you deserve so much—think of all the starving children in India!

  Having low self-worth probably explains it more than anything else. I grew up not thinking very highly of my abilities and myself. I didn't expect to be worth a lot of money. I tend to undervalue my work and myself.

◆ *What are the payoffs for keeping the status quo?* As long as I'm always struggling to keep my head above water, I don't have to face the challenge of becoming greater than my little, personal struggle. I have some fears about becoming a highly successful person, being out in the world in a bigger way. What if you climb way out on a limb and then it breaks? That's an even greater risk than clawing your way up the tree and clinging to its trunk. So I'm protected, in a sense, from bigger failure, by playing a smaller game.

  My worrying also serves to keep me focused on building my business. I have to keep choosing what's important to me. I have to be responsible and accountable. I'm practicing the policies I need to master to succeed in a bigger way. Also, there are some things I need to get cleared up before I will be ready to make it in a really big way.

  You know what I just figured out? This issue that I have been considering such a big, heavy problem is actually quite useful to me in many ways. By going through all this, I can see that looking at it in this new way will help a lot. It's a challenge I will face and learn from; why not make it an adventure, a divine comedy, instead of a morbid tragedy? It's my chance to handle my concerns about money, once and for all. You know, the more I trust and let go, the more confident I become that I can trust still more in the future.

This person worked with his problem until he was able to transform it into an opportunity. He moved his energy state from problem-solving into dream-creating. He has his eye on the clear skies now, and the dark clouds of doubt are but a veil to be drawn back, exposing the bright light behind.

As long as you stay stuck in your problem, it's very likely that your subconscious mind will send out commands to every function of your body and mind: "All right—all forces—align with the block! All forces align with the depression." The switch comes when you take over the controls and send out an overriding command: "All forces, align with the solution. All forces, set your sights on my dream!"

What's the Payoff?

Payoffs often represent an important part of our unwillingness to make a desired change or to resolve an issue that troubles us.

Payoffs are often insidious—we may have difficulty even identifying what they are—but that doesn't weaken their power over us.

Our payoffs for staying stuck can be many and varied. We may enjoy the camaraderie of the down-and-outers. We can hold a "pity party," commiserating and accumulating sympathy about how *bad* it is and how awful so-and-so has been acting. Have you ever noticed how talking about a situation may divert your attention from taking any action to remedy it? At worst, we can even aggravate the situation by dwelling on and magnifying its negatives.

Yet, we sometimes go from one person to the next, dumping our story onto anyone who is willing to carry around some of our bad feelings for us. It doesn't help them, and it certainly doesn't help us resolve our situation, either. The answer? Take care to release your energy not into puddles here and there where it will only stagnate and ferment, but into constructive channels where it can go to work for you and solve the problem.

Frequently, our payoff in staying with a problem is that we simply choose to remain safe and comfortable, rather than to take the risk of change. The appeal of a regular paycheck, pension plan, and health insurance certainly made me hesitate to leave my secure teaching position to expand my frontiers.

Another payoff might be that as long as you're focusing all your energy on outside problems, you don't have to be the main character in your own story: Someone else is responsible. Someone else is to blame. You can observe what is happening to you and just *react,* rather than *act.*

Write and Rewrite Your Story

Alan was a workshop participant who gained insight into his pattern of reacting rather than acting. I suggested that he write a short story about his life as it would be two years from now, if his problem situation remained unchanged. "I saw my future as clear as a bell," he reported after rereading his story. "I kept getting fatter and lazier and more withdrawn, and my wife kept getting angrier, more bitter, and critical. I drank more beer, and she stewed in silent protest until she exploded with rage."

"No!" he exclaimed. "I don't want my life to look like that." Alan wrote a second, parallel story about his life in two years, describing the needed changes to create it the way he wanted it.

This exercise of writing parallel stories may help you to picture the scenery along each of two diverging roads you must choose between. It also can give you the impetus you need to make your decisions for change. So take your Dream Journal now and write two stories for yourself: first, as your life will be in two years if you stay with your present problems, and second, as your life will be if you have made the needed decisions to create the life you want. Reread your writing and summarize in *The Live Your Dream Workbook.*

Get Clear and Take Action

On the other hand, perhaps the time is not yet right for you to make your change. Your payoff may be the extra time you need to adjust or to prepare yourself or other circumstances in your life. In this case, it may be advantageous to define what conditions you are waiting for and be clear about *when* the time *will* be right. Perhaps you need to take some classes, research your options, or interview others for their opinions. Is your dream greater than all your other considerations?

There's a fine line between knowing the time is not quite right and procrastinating. Whenever I have doubts about taking the next step or pausing to honor my own timing, I ask the question, "Am I supposed to go, do, be that?" I take it to my Dream Journal. I write the question at the top of a blank page and then sit quietly until the answers start to come. I have discovered that I am always provided with the clarity I need before I take action. Your subconscious mind always knows what the right decision is for you. Writing brings out the inner knowing. The key to discovering your own truth is to take the time to sort out and arrive at the solutions you know you will commit to.

CHOOSE HEALTHY PAYOFFS

Illness often serves as a faulty problem-solving technique. Temporarily, if you get sick, you don't have to be responsible. You can avoid communicating honestly or confronting an uncomfortable situation or relationship. You can take that much-needed rest, now that your body demands it. On top of that, you may be able to elicit someone else to take care of you, handle things for you, and perhaps even give you loving attention! And others will inquire sympathetically about your condition; then you can share sickness stories.

As director of a private elementary school, I initiated a way to accomplish all these goals—without the necessity of getting sick to do it. Our "wellness policy" was based on the principle of integrity. Every staff member and student was held responsible for creating his or her own state of well-being. If someone wanted to take a day off to work on their well-being, that was fine. The school was in full support of wellness, and we encouraged everyone to take the best possible care of themselves and do whatever they needed to provide healthy conditions for their bodies.

People were amazed by the freedom we made available to the children. I was often asked, "Will anyone ever *come* to school?" "Oh, yes," I always answered with confidence. Absenteeism was almost nonexistent in the school. The children and staff loved coming to school, and hated to miss a minute of it. We found that once you challenge people at a high level of integrity, they will respond at that level—and feel wonderful about themselves in the process.

Develop Your Own Wellness Policy

So here's a challenge for you: Develop your own wellness policy. Design a decorative page in your Dream Journal, and use it to write answers to the following questions:

+ How many days a year will you need to take off from work, dedicated to your well-being?

+ What will you use your days for?

+ Will you expect to be reimbursed for these days? How will you work out a way to be paid?

+ List ways in which you will reward yourself for wellness. How will you treat yourself in a special way on your well days?

+ What action will you take when body symptoms begin to send you messages that your wellness may be in jeopardy?

+ How will you enroll others in your wellness?

+ What arrangements will you make with your employees and coworkers to accommodate your wellness policy?

+ What will you do to enroll others in *their* own good health?

+ Reread your Dream Journal entries and summarize them in the workbook.

I have noticed that the only times I've ever been sick were when I was not honest about facing situations affecting me. I got laryngitis when my attempts to speak out and challenge a repressive boss failed to make an impact. If I was sick, I could not work there. Finally, I had to face the truth that that environment was not where I belonged—and leave it. I haven't had laryngitis since.

My learning from this experience was to be honest with myself and honor my own important values. Out of facing this problem, I left a job I might still be in otherwise. I opened up a whole new arena of opportunities that I never would have encountered in my old job. What a gift this has turned out to be!

Many individuals have brought wellness to triumph over illness by analyzing the payoffs of their illness and choosing more effective ways of having their needs met. Karen was dealing with the problem of obesity. When she looked at the payoffs available from being overweight, she realized she "was letting her sandbags keep her balloon from going up." Once she decided to be a light, carefree, and happy person, she began letting the excess weight fall away.

A distressing skin rash that made her feel unpresentable troubled another woman, Lynne. "What are you itching to do?" I asked her. The work she most wanted and yet feared to do involved being in the public eye. Her decision to go ahead and do it anyway marked the end of her problem with rashes.

Headaches often have the payoff of excusing people from going somewhere or doing something they don't want to do. Headaches can be replaced by a straightforward decision to honor our preferences and express them openly. We can choose to resolve the issue actively, rather than passively blocking our creative energy.

Backaches, too, may result from a person's feeling that he or she is carrying more than the fair share of a burden. Backaches can express passively, "Get off my back!" A back problem may force a person to cut down on a heavy load of obligations or to ask for needed help. Again, actively handling the situation more effectively might become the choice of preference. Some of the most powerful people I've ever met are ones who took the gift from a critical illness and turned it around.

Vacation or Hospitalization: What Do You Really Want?

Think of the last time you felt sick. What was going on in your life? In your Dream Journal workbook, write what was going on in your life at three other times you have gotten sick. For each, write what the payoff was. Did the sickness bring about the desired payoff? Would there have been an alternative way to reach that goal? What can you learn from this?

No More Problems. Now What?

Despite extensive work to get their lives in order, people frequently find themselves actively or passively sabotaging their own efforts. They catch themselves in the act of almost deliberately setting up new problems, moving backward instead of forward, throwing away the gains they have made. What can be going on? They are hard-pressed to understand.

It is a common occurrence that once we clear away the clouds and shift our focus away from solving problems, we feel a void in our lives. Something will rush in to fill this void. We'd better be ready with a plan to go forward—or else, watch out! A new problem will arise to compete for our newly freed attention.

The alternative to focusing on our problems is always to *focus on what we want.* By knowing what we want, we can:

✦ Design our day, just the way we want it.

✦ Know what we're working for and where we're going.

✦ Choose who to be with.

The quickest tool for refocusing is always the single question: What is *your dream?*

Move Into Creating Your Dream

So once you are ready to move beyond problem-solving and into creation, ask yourself the following:

✦ What do I want?

✦ When do I want it?

✦ Am I willing to take action?

✦ At what point will I definitely take action? (How bad does the situation have to get before I reach the absolute limit of my willingness to put up with it?)

✦ What possible actions could I take? (Be creative here. The more unlimited your thinking is, and the more possibilities you define, the better your chances for success will be.)

✦ What specific actions will I take, by what specific times?

✦ How will I know when I have what I want?

✦ What is my payoff in not having what I want?

✦ How will I reward myself with an equal or even greater payoff for having what I want?

A Model for Managing Payoffs and Options

On page 132 is a flow chart modeled on these questions. Once you have studied it, take a blank sheet of paper and create a flow chart of your own to help you transcend a problem situation you'd like to resolve in your life at this time.

Your Power to Turn Negatives Into Positives

What do I want?

A happier relationship with my spouse.

When? → Later. / Right now! Immediately.

Journal.

Am I willing to take action? → Yes / No

At what point will I act?

What possible actions could I take?

Set up a schedule for sharing household tasks. → When? → By Friday.

Buy theater tickets to spend a night out together. → When? → By Thursday.

Make time to talk together. → When? → Tonight.

Arrange for marriage counseling. → When? → Talk about it tonight.

Journal about it. → When? → This afternoon.

Did this work to get what I want? → Yes / No

How will I reward myself? → Enjoy the play and time together.

What will I do next to keep the progress going? → Schedule a night out every week. → Make more time to talk.

What else could I try? → Avoid complaining. / More positive communications.

THE POWER OF YOUR WORD

Reaching your dream takes motivation, determination, and effort. You will need to clear away the obstacles that have blocked you in the past. One obstacle that often escapes our awareness is the language we use.

I was once working with a class of young children when I noted how many disparaging remarks were being exchanged. Something had to be done. I initiated a discussion about the power of words we use with each other—words that make us feel better and words that make us feel bad. One little girl said, "Like when my daddy tells me to shut up—you feel *dead* when someone says that to you."

We began to make a list on the board of "Dead Words." Another little boy timidly raised his hand: "You're not going to write this." Dedicated to the lesson, I encouraged him to go ahead. "When somebody says, 'F—you,' it *kills* you." Expecting the principal to walk in any minute, I added his contribution to the board.

These kindergarten children already knew what bioenergetic research has discovered and proven scientifically: Your physical energy decreases measurably when your focus is on the negative. Yet in our everyday language, people commonly use killer phrases. A participant in one of my workshops told me, "I have been so programmed to be a negative person, and it is my constant work to turn that negativity around. I want to change this habit!"

One of my clients, Lee, seemed unaware of the damaging effects of his sarcasm. I confronted him on this "killer talk." I told him, "You know, your sarcastic remarks take the place of genuine, honest communication. Instead of really communicating, you put people down. It also often creates a barrier between us, and every time you do it, I feel like you've just put a knife in me." A change came over his presence, but I was counting on our working relationship to be strong enough to support the truth being told, even though it was painful to hear in the moment.

At our next meeting, Lee thanked me. He had never realized he used sarcasm in this way, and injuring people and creating barriers were not what he really wanted to accomplish, of course. "You already know this," he disclosed. "What I am really working on is my own low self-esteem. Thank you for helping me to see this."

The most deadly effect of killer talk is not on others, however, but on the self. When we say, "I *can't*" or "I'll *try*," we deflect the power of our intentions away from positive action and an open mind, and toward negative and limiting ideas and judgments. We see ourselves as powerless.

Imagine that I say, "I *should have* stopped at the store on the way home. We *need* milk, but I *can't stand* waiting in those *unbearable* long lines at rush hour." In these two small sentences, I have heaped guilt on myself with the loaded assumptions of the word *should,* and I have judged myself as *needy* and *intolerant.* I am left feeling wrong and ineffective.

On the other hand, suppose that I say instead, "I will go to the store for milk later, to avoid wasting time standing in line at rush hour." This is a statement that empowers me: I have viewed the situation objectively and chosen my action based on my own preferences. I feel effective and in control, and I have not cast negative judgments on myself or anyone else.

If I say to you, *"Why* don't you *ever* call me when you're going to be late? *You are* so *inconsiderate* and *thoughtless!"* in all likelihood, the way I have phrased my remarks will short-circuit our communication. You will be made to feel wrong, and your predictable response will be either to withdraw defensively or to counterattack. My accusations may seem justified at the moment, but my problem remains unresolved and in the long run I will feel, once again, frustrated and ineffective.

On the other hand, I could more carefully consider what I want to communicate. I might choose caring language that invites a response: *"I felt* concerned when you didn't call. I didn't know whether to go ahead with dinner or to wait. I thought of canceling this evening's plans, but then I was sure you'd be here soon. After wavering back and forth like this, I began feeling angry. *I want* you to know what I have been going through. *I'd like* reassurance that you care about me and are concerned about what I'm feeling."

The language we use can subtly set up our experience and determine the way we view others and ourselves. Awareness is the key to a successful experience. Practice noticing the words you choose.

Enliven Your Language, Enliven Your Life

Read the following examples to begin to notice if you are using "Dead Words" or "Alive Words."

Notice if you are using "Dead Words" such as these:

I can't...	Why didn't you...
I won't...	You *never*...
I'll *try*...	Don't...
I should have...	Shame on you!
I can't stand...	Can't you ever...
I *need*.	You *always*.
If only.	Will you *ever* learn?
It's their *fault*.	You *have to*...
We've *got to*...	But...

If you aren't careful, you'll...

Practice substituting "Alive Words" such as these:

I like.	Thank you.
I can.	Good for you!
I will.	I like the way...
I'll *do* it.	I appreciate...
I want.	Well done!
I feel.	Nice job!
I love.	I choose/choose not to.
Let's talk about it.	What do you want?

Become an observer of your language, and notice how you feel when you use "Dead Words" and "Alive Words" and how you feel when others use them with you. Practice consciously choosing empowering language. You will be amazed at the power of your own words. Review and summarize as your write in your Dream Journal and *The Live Your Dream Workbook.*

Turn Your Weaknesses Into Strengths

Now, let's examine and work with some other ideas you may have about yourself.

Make an Inventory of Your Strengths

We'll begin by using the sentence starter, *A strength I have is.* Repeat this quickly 20 times, completing the sentence with a different ending each time. Just say the first thing that comes to mind, without stopping to think or judge your responses. Here's an example:

A strength I have is I'm a great clarinet player.

A strength I have is willingness to admit my mistakes.

A strength I have is my athletic body.

A strength I have is I write wonderful letters.

A strength I have is a mature relationship with my parents.

A strength I have is my strong sense of humor.

Go ahead and explore your own strengths, counting up to at least 20 completions for this sentence. (This is a good exercise to do with a dream partner.)

Then read this next section over carefully; it has the potential to change your life.

Usually, when I ask adults to list their strengths, they mention many skills they have mastered and things they are good at doing. I have never yet had an adult list as a strength something that he or she was still in the process of developing. Yet a child will joyfully boast "I'm learning sign language!" or "I want to be an artist when I grow up." As children, we see all our potential abilities as strengths. It's a wonderful outlook that need not be sacrificed on the altar of adulthood.

Benjamin Franklin once said, "A weakness is a strength not yet developed." Go ahead grab your journal and write a quick list of 10 things you consider to be weaknesses you have. Now, here's the trick: look at each of these "weaknesses" and begin to see it not as a weakness, but as a strength in the process of being developed—a *budding strength.*

For example, a participant in one of my workshops was laid off from a long-term career position. She felt so incapacitated by fear and worry that she was unable to begin searching for a new job. Using the above procedure, she identified her weaknesses: the fear of making new contacts, of going to job interviews, of being put on the spot, of fumbling and feeling awkward and self-conscious, and presenting a miserable impression of herself and her abilities.

From these weaknesses, she wrote the following strength statements:

✦ "A strength I have is that I can go into interview situations with confidence and self-assuredly present my best self."

✦ "A strength I have is that I enjoy the opportunity to make new contacts and explore new possibilities with new employers."

"I realized I had made some arbitrary decisions about myself, and I was stuck with the consequences of them. Suddenly I knew I could instantly change those decisions—and would!" she exclaimed.

List Your Budding Strengths

So what are your "budding" strengths? Use the power of your word to turn each of your weaknesses into a strength you are now developing. Make a strength statement:

"A *strength* I have is _____."

Extend Your Srengths

When you have completed your strength statements, go on to list every negative idea you have accumulated about your appearance, your abilities, your intelligence, your cooking, your social skills, your education—any negative thought about yourself that you have. Then use a separate page in your Dream Journal. For each negative belief on your previous list, write a new, empowering strength statement. Example: "I am a clumsy, bumbling idiot" might be changed to "I am coordinated and clever." "I am terrified of talking in front of a group" could be replaced with "I am a confident, inspired, and inspiring public speaker." Be playful and daring. My guess is you'll like these new dream inspiring sentences!

Eliminate Weaknesses

When you finish this list, tear up the other lists of negative ideas. You may even want to burn the pages filled with what no longer fits your renewed self so the old notions go up in smoke!

Creating positive strength statements to replace the old negative ideas and beliefs may feel at first like wearing new shoes. Your logical mind will naturally come through with all kinds of "reasonable" arguments and objections. The old beliefs were familiar and comfortable; will the new ones ever fit? *But,* you may think, *I don't* feel *coordinated and clever! How can it be true?* Someone once advised me to view these thoughts as passing clouds in the sky. Just allow them to appear, and observe them as they move on by. In the meantime, go ahead and *be* your new, strengthened self.

One less constructive—and usually unconscious—thing we do with our negative self-concepts is punish ourselves for them. We use guilt and self-punishment to keep ourselves in line and correct our "bad" behaviors. We criticize our own egos and deny ourselves pleasure, privileges, and even basic needs, all as punishment for our own perceived misdeeds or weaknesses.

Of course, self-punishment does not work. It also robs us of vitality and aliveness and cuts us off from the reinforcing strength of feeling good about ourselves.

Always Write About Your Learning

When we punish ourselves, we turn away from the potential learning of a situation. It works far better to appreciate yourself: You did the best you knew how to do, given the circumstances and your experience to date. Your choices have led to another opportunity to learn further. *Instead of being critical, be curious.* What are you learning through this? What is the value to be derived from your experience?

Do you sometimes punish yourself? How? For what? As you progress in turning negative thoughts into positive ones, notice also when you are punishing yourself. Write about this in your Dream Journal and workbook. Write how you can accomplish your purposes by loving yourself more instead of punishing yourself.

Remind Yourself to Positivize

Write yourself some reminder cards, and post them around your working and living space:

> HOW IS THIS PERFECT?

> WHAT AM I LEARNING AT THIS MOMENT?

> DOES THE THOUGHT GOING THROUGH MY MIND RIGHT NOW SUPPORT ME IN LIVING MY DREAM?

Start shouting and chanting whatever you want to be true about yourself. Yell out in the privacy of your car affirmations that empower you, such as "I am a confident public speaker!"; "I present material in a clear, articulate way"; and "I am determined to succeed."

You are the authority for your own life. You, and you alone, are the one best qualified to make all the decisions, choices, and judgments on your life. So don't let people, places, or things get in the way of choosing what is right for you. If I perceive something as a problem, *my perception is the problem.*

When you work from the position of your strengths, you begin to live from the full array of your potential. Your life shifts from a struggle for survival to an adventure in choosing what you want. You move out of the problem-solving mode and into the creative process.

Any problem can be turned into a positive learning experience if we purposely ask ourselves, "What's the value in this situation? What is the gift? The understanding? What am I learning?" Approach your problem situations not with groans and complaints, but with a willingness to learn and receive the gift. Just say, "Oh, good! This must be perfect! Let's look at how. Might as well have fun with it." Hop over your resistance and move lightly through your next learning opportunity. You will maximize your energy and your effectiveness. Instead of choosing to be miserable, why not choose to enjoy yourself?

Are you having fun yet?

Dreamwork Checklist

❑ Keep up your reading and writing in your Dream Journal and workbook.

❑ Continue completing things and working on your Dream Plan.

❑ Write the story of your problem from the point of view of a third person.

❑ Find and receive the gift in every problem situation.

❑ Examine your problems or issues.

❑ Identify the payoffs related to an issue.

❑ Release your energy into constructive channels.

❑ Write parallel stories about how your life will be two years from now.

❑ Write about the payoffs of illness and what your alternatives are.

❑ Develop your own wellness policy.

❑ Keep asking, *What do I want?*

❑ Make a flow chart plan for getting what you want.

❑ Watch your language. Use Alive, not Dead, Words.

❑ Ask your dream partner to catch you using Alive Words and compliment you.

❑ Turn your weaknesses into strengths.

❑ Stop punishing yourself; appreciate and learn.

❑ Choose to change your focus from problems to solutions.

❑ Turn your negatives into positives; choose to move on and enjoy!

❑ Reread your writings your Dream Journal and workbook often to reinforce your learning and discoveries.

ASK JOYCE!

Q: I am living through a very painful situation right now. I just read the section titled "The Power of Your Dream To Weather The Storm." Do you think I should seek out help to weather my storm?

A: Only you can make that decision and yes, I do highly recommend seeking out a therapist whenever you know your life experiences are overwhelming and you need a place to express yourself honestly and fully. This is vital to a growing person.

   Reaching out to others is often just the step that is needed to move closer to living your dream.

Q: I have just moved to a new town and I have not made any new dreamer friends. I have a new job that I am excited about, but my friends and family are now thousands of miles away. I am not feeling as confident as I'd like and I feel like I may lose sight of my dream. What advice do you have for a dreamer who wants to stay on her dream path?

A: I truly believe that for every door that closes, new ones open. Your new life can be designed to empower and energize you. This is a perfect time for you to look at these changes as a perfect time to start a new chapter in your Dream Journal. Start off each morning by asking yourself: *What new people and new experiences do I choose to lift my spirits and take me closer to realizing my dream?* Take a few minutes and jot down your answers, then open your door and walk out into your dream life!

Q: I have a weight problem, and I spend too much time worrying about my appearance and being healthy. What advice do you have for me?

A: Is one of your dreams to be healthy, fit, and thin? Then the most important step is to reach out for help. There are many wonderful resources available if you are ready to make the commitment to this dream. Call an expert today!

Q: I think I am clear and I keep scaring myself. How can I have more courage?

A: When I first designed and facilitated the "Live Your Dream" workshops I often heard statements such as "I'm going to need a lot of courage to leave my job," "I don't know if I have the courage to tell my husband that I want to write instead of help him in his business," and "As I read your book, Joyce, I said to myself, 'Joyce, you seem to have more courage than I do.'" These types of statements brought out a reply that even surprised me when I said it! I quickly respond, "It's not courage; it's clarity!" I still believe this.

My recommendation is that you think about this notion and tell yourself the truth. Decide what your dreams are and begin to live each day accordingly, with clarity. I believe you will be amazed that having more courage is no longer an issue.

Q: I did exactly what you suggested in your *Live Your Dream* book by writing parallel stories, but my blank page is still blank. Will you give me some more ideas?

A: Blank pages can be disarming, I agree! Here are my suggestions to help get your creative juices flowing:

   ✧ Make a list of questions to ask someone who has a dream similar to yours.

   ✧ Arrange to meet with a dream partner or mentor and share the list of questions you wrote.

   ✧ Take an action step you have been putting off and reward yourself in some way.

   ✧ Make a change that will bring you new energy and keep you on the path of your dreams!

Q: I am feeling isolated right now. I am very excited about living my dream and I feel like I need more contact with other dreamers. What should I do?

A: What you could do to change your energy and current state is:

   ✧ Call a dreamer friend and set up a fun and invigorating dream partnering session right away.

   ✧ Plan to meet at a place where you will feel like celebrating the new you that is emerging.

   ✧ Take a camera to capture the two of you living your dreams.

   ✧ Before you leave, set up another dream date.

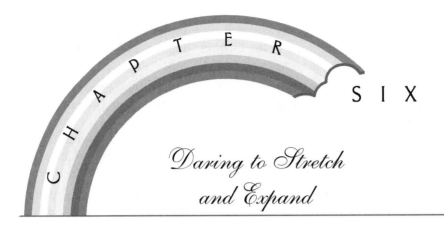

CHAPTER SIX

Daring to Stretch and Expand

*Dare: to be sufficiently courageous; to challenge;
to confront boldly; an act of imaginative
or vivacious boldness.*

—*Webster's Ninth New Collegiate Dictionary*

*M*ore stretching? Yes. Is there no end? When do I get to lie back and get comfortable and stay the same for the rest of my life? Never. I hate it! No—I love it.

The day I decided to be all I am, I became fully aware that stretching and expanding was to be a constant, lifelong process. There's always more to learn and more to become. Our only limit is our own willingness to grow.

Of course, it's important to take time off to rest, relax, and rejuvenate. But overall, if you are fully committed to living your dream, you will be working harder than ever before, enjoying it more, and having more fun than you ever dreamed was possible.

I know people who can have a good time at parties. Some people can really enjoy their night at the ballpark, an evening out, or a weekend camping in the mountains. But how many people do you know whom you would describe as 100-percent happy individuals? Who *love* their lives, and live fully, with gusto and without constraint? Who, through being who they are, are making a difference in the lives of others?

This is you, if you are continuing to stretch and expand, to fill more and more of the possibilities of your dream every day and every year. When asked, "Are you having fun yet?" what is your answer? In this chapter, we will expand *fun* to *FUN!*

This is a critical point now. You are headed toward celebration. Those new shoes are being broken in. Soon, they will feel so natural, you will run and dance freely in them. You will not only boogie, you may learn to dance the mazurka or compete in the Olympic high jump. You will extend your idea of what your shoes and you can do.

This is a point where many individuals give up, if they have not built adequate self-reinforcing rewards and supports into their program for growth. It's the point at which some participants want to sit out my remaining workshops as nonparticipants, although those who keep doing their dreamwork move forward by leaps and bounds. The steps required are not always easy—and the rewards are incredible.

So, are you fully committed to advancing your dream? Are you ready to progress to the next level, to leave behind your reticence and excuses, and to do whatever it takes?

REINFORCE YOUR LEARNING—IT'S GETTING FUN NOW!

Begin by taking stock of your progress in stretching and expanding to live your dream so far. Start at the beginning of your Dream Journal and *The Live Your Dream Workbook*, and review what you have written. As you do this, highlight, underline, and write in the margins to make notes of the actual, concrete progress you have made since you began living your dream.

Reading over your work is an important way of reinforcing the steps you have taken and the leaps you have made, both in awareness and in action. Acknowledge yourself! You—and no one else but you—have done what needed to be done to propel yourself into your own future. What changes have you made? How is your life different now? In your Dream Journal, write a summary of your "Live Your Dream" process so far. Then meet with your dream partner and read it over to him or her.

Living your dream can be a lonely process. Your dream is *your* dream, and no one else can live it for you. And it can be scary, too. In my work with private clients and groups, I have constantly been made aware how vitally important it is for people to keep acknowledging themselves for their progress and to create a strong support system for this purpose.

Recently I observed my youngest grandchild toddling her first steps across a living room filled with doting relatives. An appreciated child does not give up after one fall. You don't drop out in the middle of the race if you have a cheering squad behind you. What athlete makes it to the Olympics without a dedicated coach?

Enroll a Support System to Empower Yourself and Your Dreams

When the first edition of *Live Your Dream* was released I had organized and facilitated several support groups for the "graduates" of my workshops. The purpose of these groups remained constant: to provide support and empowerment. The name of the group changed over time from "Share the Dream" to "Together to the Top" and many other versions. Today these groups are called "Dream Circles." I also designed a guidebook for dreamers who wanted to create a support group for themselves and fellow dreamers. In Chapter 1, I recommended finding a partner to team up with to go through the entire *Live Your Dream* series. Now I recommend starting and creating an empowerment group—a dream circle.

To start your empowerment group/dream circle, follow these steps:

1. Sit down and make a list of dreamer friends you may want to invite to gather together and create a Dream Circle.

2. Read over your list and beside each name write why you would like to be in a Dream Circle with this person. (Don't be afraid to add or delete names.)

3. Create an invitation or flyer or use the following sample to provide information and stimulate interest.

An Invitation—
to be part of a Dream Circle

Who: You

Why: To free your energy to be creative!

To identify the dreams you are ready to claim.

To commit to yourself.

To share with other dreamers and join together for fun and support.

To join with others, in a safe environment, to voice your doubts and concerns.

To step into your power to celebrate the life of your dreams.

To ignite your spirit power.

To learn and choose to make celebration a habit of your life.

To declare this is the day, the month, and the year to make your dreams real!

When: (Exact dates to be determined by the host and participants.)

Where: A location perfect for dreaming (in a home or place of business).

Cost: Fee will be based on any materials and supplies needed.

4. Send out your invitation or Dream Circle flyer.

5. Choose and arrange your location.

6. Make telephone calls to confirm the receipt of the invitation and the date and time of the first meeting, and begin the bond with your Dream Partners and Circle Partners.

As the host of the first meeting, you need a timer, paper, and pens, and you need to set up the room. These responsibilities will be shared in the future.

The Dream Circle participants become effective partners in holding the constant vision of each person's dreams through the difficult times and diversions. They agree to give each other needed nudges and positive re-minders and to tell the truth with love when it needs to be heard. The emphasis is on recognizing the progress each person makes—with fan-fare, celebration, and fun.

As with most aspects of life, it is always easier to follow another person's path or walk with someone else as you accomplish or set out towards a goal. There is nothing more unsettling than to think, *Am I the only one who thinks this way?* or to feel that certain loneliness of march-ing along without anyone else in sight.

A Dream Circle supports you and your dreams by joining your dream to others. When we actively acknowledge our dreams by writing them down and joining with other dreamers, we say to the world and ourselves: "I have a dream. I am claiming my dream. My dream will come true!"

THE NEXT SHIFT IN CONSCIOUSNESS

Psychiatrists are sometimes disparagingly known as "shrinks," com-paring the science of understanding the human mind to "head-shrinking." Presumably, a person's thoughts are so immense and unwieldy that they must be shrunk down to size to impose order on them. It is probably true that we do have to contain an untamed creature within the scope of our understanding before we can assume authority over it and teach it to do what we want.

An important step in human evolution was made when psychiatry be-gan to be identified as mind *expanding*. Self-awareness is then associated with *expanding,* instead of contracting, our experience.

It is the awareness of our own inner dynamics that gives us the power of choice over our lives and the power to choose to transcend old patterns.

It is through self-awareness that we can choose to be in the stretch and expand mode now, and to make our next important shift in consciousness. Here are two stories to introduce this:

The Wretched Little Old Lady

Once upon a time there was a wretched little old lady. Each morning she woke up with the very same thought: "Do I *have to* get up already?" Then she would look outside and see the leaves the wind had blown over her walk. "Do I *have* to sweep the walk again?" she would whine. Her house had a way of getting dirty overnight, it seemed. "Don't tell me I *have* to clean again today!" she moaned. She would stare resentfully at the list of bills and taxes she *had to* pay, and the garbage that *had* to be taken out. And the leak in the roof *had* to be fixed before it rained. But the one thing she hated more than anything else was the sight of all those happy faces going to and from the playground across the street. It was more than a body could bear, seeing everyone else smiling and playing, when all *she* had to do was work and worry.

The Cheerful Little Old Lady

Once upon a time there was a cheerful little old lady. Each morning she would look outside and see the leaves the wind had blown over her walk. "Oh, good!" she would exclaim. "I can sweep the walk again! What a beautiful day for being outside!" And sure enough, her house was dirty again. "It feels so good to clean," she would think to herself. "It's great exercise." When her eye fell lightly on the list of bills and taxes to be paid, she would think how much she appreciated all the people and services she was helping to support—the trash collectors, for example. She could just leave her garbage on the curb, and it was all taken away for her. "I guess I get to learn about fixing leaky roofs next," she smiled, knowing in advance that something of value lay ahead for her in that experience. Her contented smile was reflected back in the eyes of a young passerby on the street outside.

And that's the shift we are ready to make: the shift from *I have to* to *I get to*. This simple shift, when entered into wholeheartedly, allows us to see ourselves as living completely from choice, 100 percent of the time. It replaces fear, resistance and reluctance with excitement and enthusiasm. What do you have to lose? Let's begin to put it into practice now, as you *get* to stretch and expand further into your dream!

EXPAND YOUR ENERGY

One of the most common dream deterrents you can inflict on yourself is letting things remain incomplete. This brings along guilt, lack of self-worth, lowered self-confidence, diminished energy, depression, and lethargy. Have you experienced any of these feelings lately?

Declare Your Freedom From Incompletes

In Chapter 3, you began to work seriously on a comprehensive list of completions. How have you been progressing on it? Turn now to that checklist and mark any items that remain incomplete. Explore each of these items, writing about each one in your Dream Journal and workbook. What questions do you need to ask yourself about it? What is stopping you from completing this item? What would you have to do to complete it? Take a close look at how it is occupying a corner of your attention and using your mental energy.

I used to spend months thinking and talking about how to handle this person or that situation. When I learned to deal with each thing immediately as it came up, I discovered that now I have nothing to think about except my dream! I'm no longer carrying anything along from the past. My energy is completely released to go forward.

People sometimes wait until someone dies to confront the unspoken words that remain to be communicated, deeds that were never done. We are reminded by a death how important it is to remain current in our communications and actions. But why wait? Staying current is just as important every minute and every day of our lives.

What was so amusing about Fibber McGee's closet in the old radio program "Fibber McGee and Molly"? We can't open the door of a stuffed closet without everything from the past 20 years tumbling out. But until we clean out and get rid of the unused baggage, we tend to forget that it will all fall out again, each time the door is unwarily cracked open. Once we do clean out our symbolic closets, we can open them and easily find a space for new things we acquire.

When I was working full-time and going to school, along with raising four children and remodeling our home, people used to say to me, "Gosh, you've got a lot of energy!" Many wanted to view me as a person who had been somehow specially endowed, biologically, with an exceptionally high level of energy. But there is no mystery to high energy levels—simply keep up-to-date in all your affairs and you will be constantly revitalized. Our life energy is natural in each of us. How much of your energy is free to live your dream today?

Push Beyond Excuses

Ask yourself about each unfinished item on your completion list: *How will I be closer to living my dream once this is completed?* Take a close look at any excuses that come to mind, such as:

+ I have to wait until I have the money.

+ There'll never be anyone else if I complete this relationship.

+ Someone in my family might need it someday.

+ I might fix it (or fit into it) someday.

+ If only my husband/wife would *ever* get around to it!

+ My mother wouldn't approve.

+ If I complete this, I'll have nothing left to do.

One advantage of being an educator is that I learned early on there's *always* more to learn. There are always more projects to take on, more work to do, and more people to play with. So confront your excuses head on and recognize them for what they are: just excuses. Then get back on course with: *What do I want?* Excuses or results?

Ask yourself: *What is the push that will get me through this?* Discuss it with your dream partner, letting him or her know what support you could use—a friendly reminder, praise and encouragement, assistance, a push?

FIND YOUR HIDDEN AGENDA

How consistent with your dream is the image you are putting out? Your hidden motives may be more obvious to others than your stated intention is. People in my workshops have uncovered many unstated agendas that work in opposition to their dream. Some common ones are "I am invisible—don't notice me"; "I want to be taken care of"; "I am a rock—nothing gets to me, and I can't be hurt"; "Mr. Nice Guy"; "I'll be the victim, and you rescue me"; and "I'll save you, you poor helpless victim."

I was once at a party when someone asked a friend of mine, "How do you *live* with a husband like that, who's always the life of the party, keeping everyone in stitches?" My friend replied coolly, "I *don't* live with that person. The person *I* live with comes home from work, has a beer, plants himself in front of the TV, and falls asleep. This comedian? I only see him at parties."

Old Images and New

What is your hidden agenda? Do you put out a message about yourself that is unlike your dream? What is the new image you want to put out? Write several paragraphs about this in your Dream Journal. An ideal method to evaluate yourself and monitor your growth is to record yourself on videotape, modeling both your hidden agenda and your new image and discussing how your new image supports your dream.

FINE-TUNE YOUR ENVIRONMENT

When I was decorating our new home, my husband asked, "Do you have to have those exact drapes? What difference does it make? Wouldn't these others be just as good?"

"It makes all the difference in the world," I said. "Those are the drapes that will say to me, every time I look at them, 'Yes—you *are* living your dream.'"

When you're living your dream, everything that you say is important and counts. You can't live your dream from a compromising position. Your dream demands the best of you. Every dark, dingy corner of your life makes an indelible shadow on your dream. It must be brought out into the light and cleaned.

Take a Toothbrush

You must fine-tune your life. An exercise that many people have found extremely valuable is the assignment to take a toothbrush and a magnifying glass and scrub every corner, crack, and crevice in every room of your house. It's a discipline that teaches people to see the dirt that's always been there but never noticed or attended to. It also requires taking personal responsibility for every aspect of your surroundings. You have to be willing to own all your nooks and crannies before you can know how to own anything greater.

So get out that toothbrush, and practice developing visual acuity. Challenge yourself to find more, and then even more smudges and grime—and then aggressively get them cleaned out. Take charge—it is your life you are creating!

Now take a symbolic toothbrush to the rest of your life. Scrub out any old dirt that takes up space your dream could fill. Update your completions list and begin conquering it. If it takes years to complete all this work, what better way could you be spending your time? Each item you cross off your completion list frees you to focus on living your dream.

New Beliefs for Old

Next, look back at your work from previous chapters on the habits, beliefs, persons, and things you allow to stand in the way of living your dream. Look also at the things that motivate you, as well as your values. You can use the work you've already done to create a chart of belief statements designed to move you beyond whatever is still holding you back.

Have you noticed yet that the only thing holding you back—really—is the *idea* that something is holding you back? In other words, it is *you.* So under each category (Habits, Beliefs, Persons, Things, Motivators, and Values) write five belief statements in your workbook that tell the highest truth about you, canceling out previous ideas about whatever you thought was holding you back.

Under *People,* for example, you might write, "I have loving friends who stand by me" or "people love to pay me richly for the excellent work I do." Under *Habits,* "I get up early and feel enthusiastic" or "I eat right to support my ideal weight and health, and I feel great." Under *Values,* "I see beauty everywhere I look," "My leisure time is a source of joy and inspiration to me," or "In intimate relationships, I am completely honest." Choose powerful statements that will empower you to live your dream.

Read your belief statements to your dream partner, and then continue to read them over daily, with the conviction that they are now true. These belief statements will have a very powerful effect, even though people do not always get results overnight. It's often a gradual process. Someone will say, "I was looking back in my workbook and Dream Journal at all those belief statements I wrote six months ago—and do you know, I now have everything I included in them! I hadn't realized it before this."

People most often notice that they are now interacting in a whole different way, and no longer dealing with negative people, and that the people they spend time with have changed dramatically. Helen was a woman with a number of paralyzing fears. She began using a belief statement: "I now have inner peace." Many classes and workshops later, she called to let me know, "I think I'm almost there!" Without giving it a second thought, she was relaxed and at ease talking on the phone—previously one of her most incapacitating phobias.

Alicia, a severely depressed and suicidal woman, came to see me. She began her first session stating, "I don't know *what* I want, and it doesn't really matter much anyway." As her coaching progressed, we worked together to create some new belief statements: "I love life, and life loves me," "My path becomes clearer and clearer with each step I take," and "Thank God for my amazing life!"

Protesting all the while—"I don't know what the hell good this is going to do"—she began using these belief statements daily. Alicia today is a vibrantly happy woman who travels widely, writes for several newspapers, and spontaneously shares her joy wherever she participates.

YOUR MAJOR LIFE SHIFT

Everything beyond whatever has stopped you in the past is now yours for the having. There are no more stops. Everything is there to support you in realizing your highest good, for the highest good of all.

Define Your Shift

As you actualize the belief statements you are practicing, you will find yourself making a major life shift from the person you used to be to the person you want to become. What words would you use to describe the major life shift you are making? Are you changing from keeping things in to giving and expressing yourself, or from someone who's *preparing* to someone who takes action, or from someone who takes orders to someone who gives orders? From someone who sits in the bleachers to someone who plays down on the field? From someone who takes care of others to someone who takes just as good care of myself?

Write your life shift in your Dream Journal and workbook along with your belief statements, so you can read it every day. Add the affirmation: "I'm changing—I can feel it!"

YOUR DREAM WORKSHOP

For this next section, you will need a tape recorder and a blank tape. Plan a time when you can be undisturbed and completely without distractions. Unplug the phone, put a sign on your door, or do whatever you need to do to assure yourself this solitary time. Begin by reading the following visualization into your recorder. Some background meditation music may be played to enhance the effect. Read slowly, and leave generous pauses wherever your imagination will need time for fantasizing. When you're ready, begin:

> As you work on your life shift, there is a special place you can go to build your dream. You are now going to create your own imaginary Dream Workshop. Place your Dream Journal, *The Live Your Dream Workbook,* and your pen close at hand to record your thoughts afterwards.
>
> Get into a comfortable position and close your eyes. Relax. With every breath, count to 10, relaxing further until even the hairs on your arm and the tiny muscles around your mouth and stomach are relaxed into peaceful, expectant anticipation.
>
> You are going for a walk down a tranquil country road. The road is lined with flowers, tall swaying grass, and oak trees with bending boughs overhead, as sunlight plays around their shadows. The atmosphere is wild with the fragrance of wild rose and honeysuckle, and you breathe in the fresh, sparkling air. Birds and squirrels whistle and chirp in harmony as one great, joyful community of nature's creatures. Even the dust under your bare feet feels soft and clean, and a summer breeze covers you with warm caresses. You turn onto a small path that winds up a gently sloping hill.
>
> Drinking in the beauty of your surroundings through every pore, you begin to sense that you are arriving at a special place that is all your own. You approach an opening, and you know that once you go in, you will be in a place where you can receive any information you need to create new dreams and find complete peace.
>
> You pause, aware that everywhere around you, you are being flooded and bathed in radiant white light. In the brilliance of this healing white light, all troubles diminish into insignificance, and you are revitalized and energized and filled with absolute love.

Now you are ready to proceed inside. You imagine the perfect entryway, a doorway that invites you to come inside and bask in the unlimited possibilities within. Perhaps it is a wooden or glass door, one that swings or slides open at the touch of a button or the glance of an eye. Create your own ideal door now, and go on inside.

Take a look around you: You're in a very special place. Use your imagination to make it beautiful and wonderful in every way. What are the walls made of? The floor? Are there windows? What is the view like? You turn to one side and notice an alcove specifically designed to be your own computer area. With a wave of your hand or push of a key, you can ask the computer any question. Pay close attention, as the answer is visible on the screen. It will assist you in growing in the next step of your dream. Knowing that the computer will always be there, and that you can go back to it any time you want, you move on to see what else there is.

Now notice what you are wearing. You can be anyone you want here. Choose the look that best supports your dream. You walk a little farther, into another room, your video area. Here, all things are possible, and you can use your video equipment to create yourself living your dream, right there on the screen. Turn on the life-size screen now. As it lights up, you see someone appear there. Who is it? What does he or she have to say to you? You notice a procession of people on the screen, all lining up to see you. Some of them are ones you used to think were stopping you from living your dream. But now, as each person comes up to greet you, they seem to have a gift for you or message to tell you. Allow each person to appear before you, and listen. What is the gift? What is the message? When the last person has gone on, notice if there is anyone else you would like to call onto the screen. You can call anyone you want to this magical screen. It has no limits of time or space. You can call someone from out of your past or future, or even someone who is no longer living. Ask him or her anything you want, and receive the gift of the answer. Look again. This screen has an even more special purpose: It can instantly enact and reenact your thoughts to create the ideal scenario of your dream. Suddenly you see, clear as life, the picture of you living your dream. Create a title for your very own video—see it, appearing on the screen? Watch as the plot unfolds. You *are* living your dream! Soon, you are ready to continue on. You know that your video viewing room will remain here for you, and you can go back any time you want.

Now it's time to prepare your special place for doing the work required to create your dream. Your work area will be as unique as you and your dream are. See that space now, exactly as it needs to be for you. If it needs to have a higher ceiling or a different kind of floor, build one. You're able to create anything you want, in any manner you choose. Is this the place you'd like to have a fountain, a beautiful piece of artwork, or some special plants? Would you like to bring in something from nature? Snap your fingers or wave a hand: There they are! Is there any special equipment you need? A piano or other musical instrument? Art supplies? Tools? You can have as much as you want. Place yourself in a perfect position for creating your dream. This is where you can always come to work on your dream. Now, bring in that one idea that will allow you to perfectly create your dream. Let it come through now.

Now you're ready to move into the special place nearby that is just for relaxing. As you enter this area, pay close attention to the colors, the sounds, the smells, and the feelings. What kind of furniture will you place here? How will you design the interior walls, flooring, and windows? Add anything you like to enhance its beauty and comfort. How about beautiful bouquets of flowers? Lighted candles? Magnificent music? A hot tub? A skylight?

Sit down, and see yourself resting and relaxing as never before in your life. You feel your energy returning and building. Here, your vitality is restored to 100 percent, and you feel wonderful.

Now your time in your Dream Workshop is drawing to a close. As you prepare to leave, sense all those feelings you have experienced here: the love, the comfort, the safety, the certainty, the warmth, the power of creating everything just as you want it. Know that you can always come back at any time, and you can change it any way you want, at any moment.

Now you move toward the opening and pass through the entry. The radiant light is there once again, surrounding and permeating you. You pause for a moment to soak up its warmth. Then slowly, you start back down the small, grassy way to the main road. You pass underneath the spreading branches, and the lights and shadows play on your path.

You are ready, now, to be back in your world, for you have everything you need now. As you move back into your everyday world, you take all your new vitality and new possibilities with you. You know that your Dream Workshop will always be there for you, anytime, anywhere that you choose to use it.

Experience yourself back now, in the room where you began. Give your body a long, easy stretch, and notice any sounds and smells around you. When you're ready, open your eyes. Go to your Dream Journal and workbook to write about your experience.

You can use this guided meditation to visualize your dream, restore your vitality, and regain your focus. Use it often. It will be most effective if you personalize your tape recording, tailoring the words to suit your own individual tastes. You can listen to it passively as you enter the meditative state and go to work in your Dream Workshop. With experience, you will discover that your answers really are there for you, and they begin to come with greater and greater ease.

Make Your Empowering Tape Still More Powerful

Use the other side of the tape to read your belief statements, against a background of inspirational music. Visualize your dream and paint a verbal picture, so you can listen to these valuable messages any time you feel down or angry or uninspired. You will find that you waste less and less time and energy mired in self-pity, boredom, or scattered thinking, and you can get back on the right track quickly.

ACT AS IF

Now you are ready to really stretch and expand! You've done it in your imagination; now let's try it out for real. What is your dream? How would your lifestyle or your way of being change if you were living your dream right now?

Stretch into New Possibilities

Begin today to experience yourself in a larger way. Think of something that would be a real stretch for you to try and write the statement in your workbook—and go do it. Test-drive the car of your dreams, and take a camera along to record the experience. Visit that meditative temple where you wondered if you might discover inner peace, even though you've never been anywhere like it before. Go skydiving, if that's something you always have thought of doing. Take ballet or singing lessons. Go skiing; take flying lessons. It all begins with your decision to expand your possibilities. Make the calls to set it all up.

Try out for a part in community theater; perform in a local carnival as a clown. By a wetsuit and snorkel; wear a bright red bikini to the beach; go to stores and try on outfits that embody the epitome of your dream. Try on the latest fashions or give away everything in your closet that no longer fits into your dream self. Spend time with your dream partner and ask him or her to go out with you. Do it all—or do nothing! Become the person living his dream!

Go all out. Even if you feel it's "not *you*" at first, you are expanding your possibilities and freeing yourself from old limiting ideas. Scream louder than anyone at the football game if you've always been shy and reserved. Be shy and reserved if you've always been flamboyant and carefree. Cry as you've never cried before; laugh hysterically. Yell at the television. Greet strangers with a smile and a friendly word. Make a stupid mistake and acknowledge it publicly if you've always had to be perfect. Get your act together if you've always been unruly.

Bring balance into your life. Ride a seesaw at the playground. Go skinny-dipping at two o'clock in the morning. Stand up in a crowded meeting and give a persuasive speech stating your controversial opinions. Send your poetry collection off to 23 publishers.

Stand up for what you believe, even if you're the only one who believes it. Spend an entire day by yourself, without talking to anyone, if that's something you never do. Take a trip to a place you're afraid is too far from home.

Speak in someone else's language even though you're afraid they will laugh at you. Go to a job interview for a position you think is "above" you. Run for political office. Call someone you haven't spoken to in a long time and talk about your dream. Phone someone in your family, and find a way to honestly communicate and ask for his or her support. Join a group of people who are already successful in a field you are just entering.

You take it from here. Do any or all of these things, and make up more of your own. Choose the very thing that would be most uncomfortable and do it. The way to get beyond fear is to confront that which you fear the most. Then the rest seems small in comparison. You always find out that the thing you fear is not the monster you thought it would be.

Grow Beyond Discomfort

I especially love this quote from Florence Scovel Shinn's powerful little book of affirmations, *Your Word Is Your Wand:* "I walk boldly up to the lion on my pathway and find it is a friendly Airedale." Make a list in your Dream Journal and *The Live Your Dream Workbook* of all the lions on your pathway. Then begin walking up to them, one by one, and start checking them off your list. What are the uncomfortable experiences you want to grow beyond? *Act as if* you were living your dream.

I Did It

And here's the biggest stretch of all: *For everything that happens, take ownership.* Can you find an argument to challenge this and an excuse to get around it? Undoubtedly. In his book, *Illusions,* Richard Bach tells us, "Argue for your limitations, and sure enough, they're yours." But once your life becomes about you being true to who you are, and telling your truth dauntlessly—the minute you take ownership—no one and nothing else has power over you. The powerful person, the manipulator—no one is ever controlling you. You, and not outside people, places, or things, are the sole shaper of your reality.

There's a wonderful quote from A *Course in Miracles:*

> I am responsible for what I see.
> I choose the feelings I experience.
> And I decide upon the goal I would achieve.
> And everything that seems to happen to me,
> I ask for, and receive as I have asked.

You can try this and discover the amazing results. Your perception may be forever changed.

Dreamwork Checklist

❑ Review your Dream Journal and workbook. Summarize your progress so far and share with your dream partner.

❑ Acknowledge yourself!

❑ Create a support team.

❑ Shift from *I have to* to *I get to.*

❑ Study and update complete items, and answer the questions about them.

❑ Stay current in all communications and responsibilities.

❑ Eliminate excuses.

❑ Complete all incomplete items.

❑ Expose any hidden agendas and practice developing your new image, true to your real self.

❑ Take a "toothbrush" to your life.

❑ Create and use the chart of belief statements. Read these over morning and evening, and keep them always in your thoughts.

❑ Write your major life shift.

❑ Create your own Dream Workshop tape, and use it often.

❑ Act as if.

❑ Make a fear list.

❑ Confront your "lions."

❑ Try something scary every day. Stretch your ideas of what you can do.

❑ Everything that happens, take ownership for your experience of it.

Ask Joyce!

Q: A friend told me that you had a section in a past issue of your newsletter titled "Just Journal! Pssst! Rumors are Flying…and They're All About You!" Will you please send me a copy of it?

A: I'd love to! Here it is:

Where do these rumors come from? Why, from your pen of course! Penning rumors about is a delightful, magical way to light up your dream or give it some fire, and it often brings amazing results. It is fun to make up your own outrageous rumors. Try it! Go ahead, don't be shy. When you are done, notice if you have a change in attitude. Don't forget to tell your Journal all about how you feel. Here are some ready-made rumors for you to take to the limit—or you can make up your own!

1. My dream of owning my own business is now a dream come true.

2. I hired a personal trainer and the results are fabulous.

3. My book is hot off the press and Oprah has already sent me an invitation to be on her show.

4. I wrote a successful screenplay, which turned into an Academy Award–winning movie.

5. I am sending out invitations to my wedding next week. Guess where we're going on our honeymoon?

Call someone and read what you have written to him or her. It will stretch you into outrageous thinking and is also a very empowering exercise.

Q: You recommend that I organize a group for myself. This is a totally new concept for me. What is my first step?

A: Sit down and make a list of why you want a support group (Dream Circle). Now, read some of the reasons I think they are necessary and fun.

- ✧ To share.
- ✧ To create.
- ✧ To ignite.
- ✧ To focus.
- ✧ To discover.
- ✧ To celebrate.
- ✧ To learn.
- ✧ To laugh.
- ✧ To commit.
- ✧ To meditate.
- ✧ To activate.
- ✧ To join.
- ✧ To journal.
- ✧ To practice.
- ✧ To align.
- ✧ To identify.
- ✧ To remember.
- ✧ To begin again.
- ✧ To dream storm.
- ✧ To motivate.

- ✧ To relax.
- ✧ To refresh.
- ✧ To visualize.
- ✧ To grow.
- ✧ To inspire.
- ✧ To experience.
- ✧ To imagine.

- ✧ To improve.
- ✧ To express.
- ✧ To be yourself.
- ✧ To claim your dreams and make them real.
- ✧ To imagine.
- ✧ To dream!

But please always remember that a Dream Circle is not the place:

- ✧ To complain.
- ✧ To dump.
- ✧ To process.
- ✧ To problem-solve.
- ✧ To coach or counsel.

- ✧ To meddle.
- ✧ To rehash the old.
- ✧ To gossip.
- ✧ To gripe.
- ✧ To be anything other than real!

After you have spent some time thinking and deciding if you want to create a Dream Circle, your next step may be to start out by making a list of your dream friends. Good luck!

Q: I love the question, *"How much of your energy is free to live your dream today?"* Unfortunately, my answer is about two percent. I know people, places, and things that have nothing to do with me living my dream often deplete my energy level. How can I change this?

A: Start off with these steps:

Section out a few pages in your Dream Journal and write down what your focus is for at least a week. Ask others to help you identify how you spend your time and use your energy. Record their observations. Then reread with a red pen in hand. Cross out any use of time that depletes your focus and energy.

Now make a list of dream steps and the necessary daily tasks to reach for and realize your dreams.

Q: I have never considered myself to be a person who makes excuses but after I read the section *"Push Beyond Excuses"* I had to admit I was an excuse-maker. I need a push now and then. Should I hire you as my dream coach?

A: Absolutely! If you're ready to make a commitment to realizing your dreams and know you want a coach I'm always excited and available to align with you to achieve what you are ready to accomplish. The easiest way to contact me is through my Web site and to sign up for a Hotline Session to discuss your dreams. My Web site is *www.joycechapman.com.*

Q: I don't think I have a hidden agenda, but now I am curious. Could I have a hidden agenda and not be aware of it?

A: Well, I have good news and bad news. The good news is that it may be time to ask your friends, family, and dream partner to tell you if they think you may be operating from a hidden agenda. The bad news (but really not so bad) is that you will have to acknowledge whatever they tell you and then change and move forward to your dream.

Q: I am astounded by viewing a video feedback session of myself, how much I have changed! I almost didn't recognize myself. I would not have believed this possible. It was a terrific assignment and was a real milestone for me. How can I make sure I don't forget the learning?

A: Thank you! It is an incredible assignment, isn't it? With some dreamers I tell them to take a picture of themselves the day they decide to live their dream and then take another picture after one month, three months, and six months—and to see if they can recognize the face that looks back at them. What you are seeing in your videotape is an empowered person who is focused and energized at life.

Q: I am about to start the book and workbook for the second time. My first partner and I did okay, but now I want to learn to be a highly skilled Dream Partner! What tips do you have for me?

A: The following tips should help you!

- ✦ Prepare, prior to your first meeting, in order to eliminate a lack of focus.

- ✦ Meet/share/set up a schedule for each month's support and empowerment.

- ✦ Model good dream partnering at all times:

  - ✧ Listen.

  - ✧ Practice taking notes as you listen. This habit will help you stay focused on the task.

  - ✧ Only give input when asked or your Dream Partner requests your feedback.

  - ✧ When/if you disagree or your opinion differs, say, *"I do not agree with that* _____ *(thinking, idea, plan, belief, etc.)."* Then ask, *"Would you like to know what my position is?"* If your partner says yes, be totally honest and share your viewpoint. (Be very conscious they are *your* views and given for support and empowerment. Do not judge.)

    ✧ Stay focused on your partner's stated and claimed dream(s).

    ✧ Take your commitment to your Dream Partner very seriously.

✦ At the end of each month evaluate if it is and will be beneficial for you to continue partnering.

Q: I often notice that days and weeks pass and I haven't done any of the work I need to do to realize any of my dreams. I want to stretch and change. What question can I ask myself to empower myself to shift into becoming an actualized dreamer?

A: Every day ask yourself: *What am I scheduling time for today that will bring me closer to realizing my dreams?* Then write your answer. You may want to enroll your dream partner to remind and nudge you often.

    I also recommend that you:

✦ Make a list of the next daring steps to take to realize your dream.

✦ Take a blank calendar for the current month and write a dream step you know will challenge you and that you can achieve for each day.

✦ Never go to bed until you have reviewed your dream work for the day or have added what is for tomorrow's to-do list.

✦ Let your dream partner know what you experience because of your commitment to realizing your dreams.

Q: In Chapter 6, you stress the importance of having a support group called a Dream Circle. What are some of the suggestions you have that my group could follow?

A: The following list should be helpful to you:

✦ Have a discussion.

✦ Pose a question to your Circle members and listen to their responses.

✦ Share your journaling pieces and what you are learning.

✦ Discuss and plan an outing together.

✦ Share an inspirational quote, story, book, experience, and so on.

✦ Team up and interview each other.

✦ Share some of the work and play time that you and your dream partner have been experiencing with a new partner.

✦ Practice a presentation and ask for feedback.

✦ Videotape yourselves and critique each other.

✦ Bring something you have completed to share.

✦ Share a realized dream and plan a celebration.

Q: I just finished reading *Live Your Dream* and I am very excited about a Dream Circle. I do have one concern, and I hope you'll answer the following question: What should I do if you doubt the reality of my Dream Partner's biggest dream?

I do understand the importance of allowing each individual to define and discover what he or she is truly going to commit to and I have this desire to challenge and question.

A: This is a very important question.

I have learned, through my years of teaching, coaching, and facilitating, the value of supporting and empowering each individual to realize his or her dreams (by providing each individual with the opportunity to discover for themselves what they are willing to work on and commit to bringing into reality with lasting results).

Also, use dream partnering to offer and encourage your partner to seek out coaching or counseling when you find yourself wanting to help or give advice that would require an expert's advice and/or counsel. Remember to concentrate on your own work and bringing *your* dreams into reality.

Keeping the Dream Alive

Life is a daring adventure, or nothing.

—Helen Keller

From dream to reality, this has been an adventure. And this is only the dawn in your future of dream living. Look at what you have become in the process of building your dream. The face you now see in the mirror is the image of an empowered being. Your fears have faded, replaced by a sparkling new motivated personality. You *are* your dream.

To keep creating tomorrows filled with happiness, achievement, accomplishment, and satisfaction, begin in this moment to say what you want and to reward yourself for every thought and act you take to bring it about. Exercise determination to shift your energy whenever your thoughts and actions take a turn away from actively supporting your dream.

Stretch until your comfort zone *encompasses* living your dream. People who arrive at this stage frequently report that, as their dream is more and more a part of their daily reality, abandoning it is harder than moving forward. Avoiding making the call is now more difficult than facing the possibility of rejection.

It all matters will become the phrase to help and empower you when you have made the firm decision to live your dream. You know every action, decision, and choice you make must be congruent with living your dream.

When new dreams come along, begin a Dream Board without delay. And be a courageous dreamer. Living your dream is simple—but it's not always easy. All it takes is for you to decide that's what you're going to do, no matter what. Give yourself a standing, gold-embossed personal invitation, such as the one pictured here on page 164.

*You Are Cordially Invited
To the Event of Your Lifetime*

Live Your Dream

*Become All You Can Be
Achieve All You Are Capable of Achieving
Fulfill the Ultimate Purpose of Your Life*

Come As You Are

Time: Starting Immediately

Place: Right Where You Are

Please Bring: The Best of Yourself

R.S.V.P. - A.S.A.P.

Throughout the book I have encouraged you to go back and review work you have done previously and record the thoughts you have had about previous experiences. Reviewing what has happened and learning to think about things in a new way are important to assure that you keep growing to new levels instead of just repeating old patterns. We keep our old programmed perceptions until we make a conscious decision to see things differently.

Examining and questioning our perceptions may draw us into a whirlpool of fear, anger, and guilt. But by moving through it, we come out on the other side with the freedom to let go of faulty thinking, choose new thoughts more in alignment with our dreams, and release our own inner creativity. And by reviewing your successes and the progress you have made, you give yourself valuable reinforcement. You come to appreciate clearly *how* you have created exactly what you wanted. You are a powerful creative being! When you choose to create your dream—and keep choosing that—you can have it!

So, as a brief summary of the "Live Your Dream" process, first define your dream. Ask always: *What do I want?* Then decide to claim and live your dream. Take a look at your beliefs, values, and habits, and replace old ones with new ones that will empower you. Define the steps and specify dates for completing your dream work. Design your life to motivate and support your newly claimed dream and your new values and goals. Turn whatever happens into an opportunity for growth: find the gift, and look for the learning. Keep stretching beyond limited ideas of what you can do. And finally, get support from others and support yourself by rereading and updating your Dream Journal and workbook and by using the techniques introduced in this book. In other words:

+ Define and claim the dream.

+ Clear away obstructions and be clear about your dream.

+ Cultivate a winning attitude.

+ Take inventory and take charge.

+ Turn negatives into positives.

+ Dare to stretch and expand.

+ Do the work to keep the dream alive.

+ Live and celebrate yourself and your dream!

STAYING ON TRACK

As you move into the culminating lap of your current "Live Your Dream" cycle, here are some questions designed to bond your progress firmly in place. Write the answers in your workbook and summarize in your Dream Journal.

+ What makes my heart sing?

+ In what ways has the definition of my dream changed since I began reading this book?

+ What is my Dream Statement now?

+ What is the most important thing I have learned about myself from writing in my Dream Journal and workbook?

+ What new habits lead me to realize my dream?

+ What new beliefs are making my dream a reality?

+ What changes in me have resulted from my work on completing things?

+ What remains for me to complete? What is my plan for completing each item I've listed?

+ What issues, situations, and relationships remain that need to be resolved or dealt with so that I can live my dream?

♦ Who are the people who are empowering me to live my dream today?

♦ What are the other empowering forces in my life?

♦ What is the biggest stretch I've made so far?

♦ What additional stretches will I make?

♦ What is the single most important thing I need to do to keep myself on track with realizing my dream?

♦ What clues can I pick up from my mood or thought patterns to help me notice when I am or am not living my dream?

♦ What are the greatest personal rewards I receive from living my dream?

♦ What contribution will you be making to the world by claiming your dream?

WRITING IN YOUR DREAM JOUNAL IS THE ANSWER. WHAT IS YOUR QUESTION?

Much of the work you have been doing has been designed to move you beyond the problem-solving morass, on to the creative *process.* So rather than "paralysis through analysis," you bring change by taking action. Rather than tackling your problems one by one, within the old structure and format that limited you in the first place, you can step out beyond where you are and *create a new reality.*

Writing in your Dream Journal and *The Live Your Dream Workbook* is one of the most valuable self-help tools you can use as you choose to model your life in the direction you want it to go. Over the years, clients and friends have often joked about me, saying, "No matter what's going on in your life, Joyce will suggest that you write about it." It's true. No one else can answer your questions with the truth that comes from *your* heart. Do you recall the line from Shakespeare's *Hamlet,* "To thine own self be true"? The direction you receive from within is the most genuine direction you can receive.

So many people have warmly acknowledged, "By your encouraging me to keep a Dream Journal, my life is completely different now. It works!" No other way provides such a powerful means of integrating past experiences and using these insights to mold your future. Your Dream Journal is your strongest counsel and your truest advisor. It is your therapist, teacher, advocate, confidante, and best friend.

The great Nobel Prize–winning physicist Albert Einstein once said that he would begin to worry about mankind if we ever stopped keeping journals.

A successful professional woman named Phyllis wrote the following words about her experience with such writing:

> Scared witless by the strong affirmation of my writing ability at a writers' conference four years ago, I froze. For nearly two years, I could write nothing. Then I heard about Joyce's "Journaling For Joy" workshops. An introductory session convinced me this would be my key, and I joined a weekly group. Now I have eight-hundred spiral notebook pages filled to the brim—and more coming. I am nearly ready to prepare my work for publication. The safe, nonjudgmental environment of this group unlocked doors that had remained closed for so long.
>
> The process has allowed me to be deeply in touch with my feelings. I am so much more aware of everyone and everything around me. The biggest change it's made in my life is that now I am able to *write* my *feelings*. It has put me in touch with the real wellspring of my inner self.

CHOOSE YOUR TOPIC—AND WRITE TO KEEP YOUR DREAM ALIVE

There are many journaling techniques that may be useful in your future dreamwork. The following sections contain suggested topics that you can look through at any time. I recommend that you choose the topic that speaks most directly to whatever issue you are dealing with. These writing ideas can be used over and over to bring you to the clarity you'll need, and want, to fully embrace living a dream life! Here are some guidelines to follow:

- ✦ Get your Dream Journal.

- ✦ Find a quiet place.

- ✦ Choose an environment that is conducive for your journaling.

- ✦ Settle in comfortably.

- ✦ Choose whatever issue or topic is important right now.

- ✦ Read the section of your chosen topic.

- ✦ Close your eyes, and let your feelings and thoughts flow.

- ✦ When you have an insight, gently open your eyes and write it down.

- ✦ After you've written your entry, reread it and give yourself feedback.

My Dream's So Big. Where Do I Start?

First, give yourself permission to be outrageous in your thinking! Write a list of 50 actions you might take to move yourself closer to realizing and living your dream. Then create a cluster diagram, as a visual picture showing how one action might lead to others. Here's a diagram done by a man whose dream was to become instrumental in improving the quality of education in the school his children attended:

Actions to Take

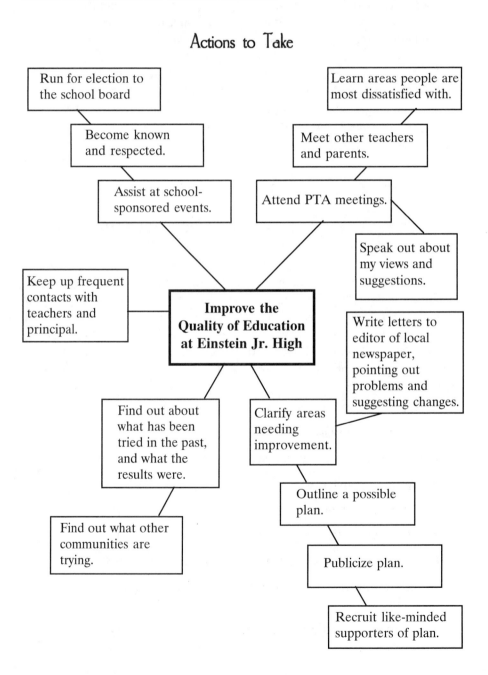

Is There a Way to Do/Have All I Want?

What exactly *do* you want? Write each idea on a single page, and plot your steps for achieving it. Then spread out all your pages in front of you and consider how they might fit together. Will you pursue several of your dream steps simultaneously? Does it make sense to finish one before you begin work on another? How much time and effort need to go into each? What approach will you take? What do you *really* want?

Why Is It Important to Me to Live My Dream?

Write answers to the following questions in your Dream journal and summarize in *The Live Your Dream Workbook:*

✦ What's it going to be like to be a person fulfilling my dream?

✦ What will the benefits be?

✦ Who will be empowered by my realizing my dream?

✦ How will this affect me?

Is your dream large enough to absorb all your energy, to command all your imagination, to use all your resources, and to impact the world in a significant way? Compare this state of being to just getting by, purposelessly. Why *is* it important to realize your dream?

How Can I Be Sure What My True Gifts Are?

Imagine that you have been drifting, lost at sea for several days and not knowing which direction to steer your little lifeboat. Morning dawns, and you see that overnight you have come within view of a tiny tropical island. As you draw near, you recognize it to be the very island where the wise sages you have been seeking reside. You have been searching for answers; you will find them here.

Write your own fantasy story in your Dream Journal and summarize it in *The Live Your Dream Workbook*. Acknowledge and embrace the answers that are revealed. First, you might like to read the example that follows. A woman named Susan wrote this story to answer her question of whether to devote her life to expressing her creative talent or not.

The woman eyed the men on the shore with some trepidation. A tall, majestic man came over to assist Star with the docking of her raft.

"We heard you were coming, and we have prepared a place for you," he said. No one seemed affected by her arrival, so she followed her newfound guide. Walking among the trees, groups of men were visible, working at various tasks—tanning hides, building rafts, and stringing beads.

"What have you come for?" the guide inquired.

"It is time for me to be in the light and to find my gift," she responded. "Who should I talk with?"

"What is it you'd like to know?" he asked.

"I want to know what to do."

The guide looked at her intently and replied, "You have been given a gift—a gift of creativity. Do not ask *how* or *why*. Just begin. Did you think you would be asked to justify yourself?"

Star found herself laughing at the ridiculousness of the idea, as her guide reached over and put his arm around her shoulder. He continued, "I will give you my cloak of freedom, and you will then remember." Star could not believe that only a few moments ago she had felt as if she were in bondage. For in this new certainty she was now released.

She wondered if she should ask. "I also came with a question for your wise one."

His smile revealed his sparkling white teeth. "First, a bath in the crystal waterfall . . . then on to more truth."

Star glanced around and found herself alone in the most beautiful secluded spot she'd ever seen. Ferns, trees, and flowers of all colors and scents bloomed around a crystal-clear pool fed by a waterfall. She wondered if she was dreaming as she glided into the pool. Feeling supported and lifted up by the water, she floated and paddled around effortlessly.

When she finally emerged refreshed and had pulled her clothes back on, her new friend suddenly reappeared. "Now?" she asked.

"Yes—now," he replied. They walked up a sloping path between two enormous boulders. Looking past her friend, Star could see an old woman seated on a rock, feeding a deer.

The old woman looked up and smiled. "Why does everyone here seem to accept me and love me?" Star wondered. She said, "Hello. I have a question still in my mind, and yet it does not seem to fit—here."

"Ask it," was the old woman's reply.

"What am I to do about money?"

"Do you *see* it?" the old woman asked.

"Yes."

"Then it's yours. No more darkness. Only light. Choose light."

"And remember this experience," said the woman in a kindly manner. Star left with a knowing she would always be free to follow her heart.

✧◆✧

WHAT DO I DO WHEN MY RESPONSIBILITIES ARE DRAGGING ME DOWN?

Most people have been trained to be critical, accurate, organized, logical, and responsible—not creative. Creativity was that little extra that it was always nice to have, although the main emphasis was on discipline and results. The focus on *structure* rather than *expression* can easily drag us down. With imagination, however, we can focus on creative expression while continuing to operate within the required boundaries.

For example, take the way many people approach the festivities of a holiday season. "Ugh!" they groan. "All those gifts to buy and events to plan for. How can I possibly manage all these added demands on my already-busy schedule? It gets more overwhelming every year." The (self-imposed) trap is rigid, and the focus is firmly set upon resistance and struggle.

Imagine the alternative approach now: "I just *love* buying presents—the special thought that goes into selecting just the right gift for each individual. Decorating my home, for me, symbolizes decorating my life with my dream. I love expressing myself in this way." This person has chosen an uplifting, creative approach rather than a dragged-down, burdened approach.

What choices are available to the person taking the first approach? That person might: 1) skip celebrating holidays altogether, becoming more honest about his or her true feelings about them; 2) change to the second approach, focusing on the positive instead of the negative aspects of holiday preparations; 3) continue indefinitely having very unpleasant experiences of the festivities.

When you feel dragged down, your choices are the same. Explore what you want by writing at the top of a new page: What will I change? How can I introduce creativity and flair into my approach to this situation?

James wrote the following response to these questions:

This annual report is always such a chore. How could anyone enjoy preparing it? Well, let's see…is there *anything* about it that is fun? I know one aspect of it that I really hate—the pressure that builds up from leaving it until the last week before the board meeting. That's one thing I sure could change.

Another thing that makes it impossible is trying to get all the facts and figures together from so many scattered, disorganized sources. The process would be much easier if I start out by collecting all the files and having the information I need to work with right at my fingertips.

It's going to be a challenge to change my approach here, though. *Fun?* Well, anything's more fun when I'm doing it with Angela. Wonder if she'd be willing to help? And the new computer spread sheet may make it easier, too. I do like its added capabilities. Maybe I'll try drawing up some special graphics, to spice up the report some.

I know! In the revenue section, I'll create a colorful chart that highlights the benefits of the new sales strategies I introduced last season and make some further recommendations. Before long, it will be evident to everybody that my ideas could play a much bigger role in making company policy decisions. That is what I really want. Preparing an impressive annual report might be a good idea, after all!

James has outlined several changes he will make. He explores his difficult task until he arrives at a way to associate the job with a purpose that is important to him. And he introduced several new ideas for approaching the task with creativity and flair. Note how he has transformed an odious task into a stimulating opportunity in a single, brief writing session!

How Will I Handle Fear?

Pretend that you are hiring an expert to advise you on how to handle your fear. Write your answers to the following questions in your workbook:

✦ What is your fear about?

✦ What are you afraid of?

✦ What is the worst possible outcome?

✦ If your fear is on the surface, what lies underneath?

✦ Is the fear truly about the present experience, or does it gain power by evoking some related past experience?

✦ How is your fear protecting you?

✦ How could you be safe as you move beyond your fear?

✦ If someone else were telling you about this fear, what advice would you give him or her?

✦ What can you do to get out of your fear and into your creativity?

Now write 15 suggestions the expert might give to you, based on the understanding he or she has obtained from your answers in your Dream Journal and summarize in your workbook. Repeat this writing exercise whenever a new fear "appears."

Is It Always Going to Be This Hard?

Write a "poor me" story, exaggerating your hardship to its extreme, even to the point of humor. After you have reread your story you might like to make a cartoon drawing illustrating your plight just for fun.

Explore what you mean by "hard." Instead of nonproductive worrying, change your question to: What's it going to take, and am I *willing to do whatever is necessary?* What if there is no "quick fix" available, and you have no choice but to stay with it? What is your realistic assessment of what is required? Ask your dream partner to support and remind you of your newly claimed attitudes.

HOW CAN I GET RID OF MY ANGER?

Many people today who have done some self-healing work have arrived at an oversimplified conclusion. They say very convincingly to themselves, "What's done is done. I forgive it, I release it, and I let it go." This statement contains the seed of truth, but I find that all too often, it is just not enough. And it can be self-deceptive, as no amount of good intentions can cover up real feelings that remain unexpressed.

Permanently getting rid of our anger usually requires that we get in touch with and express the hurt that lies at its source. When you are ready to understand and release your anger, write this question at the top of a blank page: What's underneath my anger? What is the hurt that needs to be expressed?

You may prefer to begin writing out your anger and your fury or rage. (I often recommend purchasing a separate journal and calling it your *Anger Journal*. Choose a color such as red to illustrate its purpose.) Getting these feelings out in the open may be exactly what you need to do first. Be sure to continue, uncovering the unexpressed pain.

Here is an excerpt from the writing of an angry teenager named Gina. Note how she has used it to work from her anger, to her pain, to her learning.

> I hate it! He can't do this to me! Damn! I won't let him do this to me! He told me he loved me! *Me!* Now he's off with somebody else. And I love him—at least I *thought* I loved him. Maybe I hate him, now. What a fool I feel like, falling all over him, believing every word he said. Now I find out it all meant nothing! I'm embarrassed in front of my friends.... Most of all, I hate to admit to myself I could make such a colossal mistake. I should've known better.
>
> I suppose the signs were there. But I didn't want to see them. I preferred to believe he was just busy, or tired. I needed him to love me. That's what hurts. I needed **it**, and I turned my needing into pretending that he did, giving up my good judgment, and fooling myself.
>
> I need to be loved. It hurts to be burned. It hurts to be alone. It's painful to admit my needy feelings.
>
> Crying helps....

There's learning for me here. I'll never betray myself for any guy again! I *don't* need love like that! In fact, I want to *want* love, not *need* it. I can live with myself, but I can't live with fooling myself. That's my truth!

HOW CAN I GO TO SLEEP WITH THESE UPSETTING THOUGHTS ON MY MIND ?

The following story unfolded for me as I sat quietly contemplating and seeking an answer to this question:

Once there was a remarkable Indian brave who, from sun passings beyond the far horizons of his memory, was told by his father, "A child is to be kissed and loved before falling into sleep; this is the way of our people."

It was the custom of this boy's tribe that each child, at birth, was presented with an oval-shaped stone with a surface as radiant as the sunlight itself. Peering into it was like seeing through to the depths of a sparkling clear stream unrippled by the faintest sigh of the wind.

This precious stone given to the newborn child was placed in a pouch of the softest leather, to be worn around his neck as an amulet for the duration of his days under the sun and the moon.

Each evening, in the warm glow of the flickering campfire, the father of this infant child would gently remove the stone and examine it closely. Then he would polish away from its surface any blemishes or scratches or smears it might have accumulated during the boy's brush with the forces of pain or hardship that day. Only when the stone was once again as clear and transparent as the love beaming from his father's eyes was it returned to the leather pouch, a shining companion to accompany the young child into the world of the dream.

As the boy grew in years and experience, he was diligently instructed by his father until, one day, he was judged old enough and trustworthy enough to become the caretaker of his own stone. Never a mar or a scratch was allowed to remain on the stone's surface from one day to the next, and so its interior depths were forever protected from the disturbances of scratch upon scratch.

At the very heart of the stone, a soft pool of light could be seen. From it, the clear, pure, undistorted image of the boy's own soul was reflected back to meet his steady, unfaltering gaze. The brave grew up to be a great, wise chieftain and leader of the people.

The events of a hectic or distressing day can easily mar the surface of your "precious stone" and cloud your vision of that shining self inside. Scratches and gouges must be polished away each day to keep your vision from becoming lost or damaged and to preserve the bright, clear image of yourself.

Take your imaginary stone in your hand now and examine it closely. How would you write your stone's story of this day? What chisels chipped away at your stone's surface today? What hammers pounded at its core? What gouges and blasts did it absorb or fend off? What forces of tension wrenched at it? Draw a diagram of your stone's disfigurement, labeling each incident of distress. Write an account of all the disturbances of your stone's day. Write whatever you need to say to "get it off your chest."

Then, looking at your diagram and reading over your writing, ask yourself: *How will I use this? What did I learn? What will I do?* On your diagram, mark the action or thought that polishes off the scratch left by each incident of the day.

Conclude by writing a statement for yourself that begins, "Now that my stone is polished once again, I see myself as clear and free. I see...."

When You Don't Like the Way Things Are

When you don't like the way things are, write about your current state in your Dream Journal and workbook. Then go to work on it: How is this *perfect* for me? What am I learning? Don't give up until you can answer these questions in a way that gives you a new insight. It may not come right away, and it may be unexpected, but eventually the insight will always be there.

When You Feel Dissatisfied

When you feel as if there is something you want and aren't getting in your life, ask yourself what you want. Then write a list of times when you have had just that. Ask yourself what patterns there are in your list: *Have I been taking action to get what I want lately? What situations must I put myself in, to experience joy (money, fun, freedom, or whatever it is you want)?* Discuss what you are experiencing and learning with your dream partner.

What If My Present Reality Doesn't Match What I Want?

If you still don't feel at peace with yourself after writing in your journal, ask: Do I want to *rewrite* this, to introduce a new sense of peace and new understanding?

A young client whose mother was an alcoholic felt devastated by the way his 10th birthday had turned out. After he had written all about it, he was still feeling a great deal of pain. I asked him to write, side by side, the ideal story of how he wished his birthday had turned out. Almost immediately, he realized that his disappointment stemmed from the mismatch between his two stories. He jumped to conclude: "Next year, I think I'll just let my birthday be like any other day. I won't expect so much. Then I won't be so miserable. But first, I'm going to read what I wrote to my mom and see what she says."

This boy had demonstrated an invaluable insight, one that takes many people a lifetime of bitter experience to arrive at: He decided to be responsible for the mismatch between his ideal expectations and the way things were. He was learning to take responsibility for the feelings and thoughts he had about what happened to him, instead of experiencing himself as a helpless victim of circumstance.

Whenever you experience a mismatch between your expectations and the way things are, first write about what is occurring and then record all your feelings about how things are. Then write your ideal scene: What expectations and hopes do you have? Review your two writings and conclude with a summary statement that assumes responsibility for creating what you want.

How Do I Fit My New Self Into My Existing Reality?

As you progress toward a fuller and brighter expression of living your dream now, you may find yourself changing faster inside than your environment and the people and circumstances outside you are. Although this mismatch may feel frustrating and exasperating, it actually represents just another opportunity to keep focusing on what you want and where you're going. Keep cleaning up, clearing out, and moving forward—realizing that some changes may take longer than others.

Write about the discomfort you're experiencing. How does it feel? What do you feel like doing on impulse? What concrete plans can you make for achieving the result you desire? Review and update your Dream Plans. How are you doing at meeting your projected deadlines? Does your schedule reflect what you are committed to achieving?

Why Is My Past So Important?

Can't I just forget it, and get on with my life? This kind of question often surfaces when we come up against some block from the past that is stopping our learning today. Everything about us is based on our past, so the value of uncovering our past is to help us understand our present and release our future from the grip of the past.

Ask yourself the following questions: *What from my past is blocking me from moving forward today? What would I choose to do if there were no blocks?* Write in your Dream Journal and summarize in your workbook: "The strengths the past has developed in me" and "The necessary learning my past has afforded me."

As you learn from your past experiences, allow new questions to surface, continuing to lead to expanded understanding. Simply remain open, write whatever question slips into your conscious awareness, and sit receptively as you allow a response to be formulated, leading to your next insight. The information that bubbles up from your subconscious mind is a vast resource for self-understanding that is always available whenever you invite it to come forward.

WHEN YOU WANT TO HEAL PAST PAIN

Here's an exercise to take this idea further: Write a letter to your mother, father, grandmother, grandfather, or whoever took primary care of you as a child. Tell her or him what you would have liked to receive. Create in your letter the exact feelings and experiences you wanted when you were a child.

Paint the picture as if it was actually happening. Let yourself feel what you wanted to feel then—really feel those feelings. You can heal past hurts by replacing them with new pictures in your mind. Imagine your caregiver gently saying to you, "That is exactly what I wanted you to have. I really did."

Write a letter to your father or a secondary caregiver or other authority figure, following the same instructions. You need never mail these letters (unless you choose to); the main healing work you will be doing is for yourself and your own memories. You may also want to share your learning with your dreamer friends.

WHEN YOU'RE READY TO COME TO PEACE WITH YOUR PAST

You are a product of all the experiences you have ever had and people you have known—plus the thoughts and beliefs you have formed about them.

Your relationship with any significant person or event from your past can be renegotiated today. But, you say, there's so much I just can't remember. I've *tried,* but it was all so long ago. We look for a big flash of enlightenment, but more often our understanding comes to us in little sparks, once we sit down and start to light the fire.

One effective technique for accessing material from your past is to begin writing stories of your childhood. Write as if you were going through your life as a picture album. In fact, if you have an old photo album, use it. Write a story about each picture that seizes your attention.

Don't stop with simply writing the story. Read over what you have written, and ask yourself: *What did I learn from this person and this experience? What am I learning now from this memory? How have these incidents in my past shaped me to be the person I am today?* Write your response.

Each time you write, new memories will present themselves—always, I've discovered, at the very moment you are ready to deal with them. Your stories will reveal in a capsulated way the impact each important person in your family and your background had on you. Let your stories lead you to discover the purpose each person had in being in your life and what that person came into your life to assist you in learning.

Whenever you come to a period where you were in conflict with another person or felt misunderstood by someone, follow up your story of it with a parallel story written from *that person's* point of view, as closely as you can imagine it would be.

You become responsible for your memories when you re-create them. You begin to understand your learning and how these events helped to shape you and your ideas. You make the transformation from the incomplete story to the story that becomes complete and perfect.

When You Have Strong Feelings

Write in your Dream Journal whenever you have strong feelings. Follow up emotional events by recording them and taking a closer look at what was going on. Strong feelings are a vital link to your creative energy, waiting to be released.

Whenever you write in your Dream Journal, make it a practice never to stop with just telling the story. Always continue on to write what your *feelings* are about it. What was the emotion tied to it? How did it make you feel? How did you feel about yourself? If it's an upsetting situation, or if you feel anger or anxiety, be sure to write about that fully. How do you feel now? If you've stirred up some sadness, do you want to just have it for now, or is there some action you need to take? Ask yourself: *What does this writing invite me to do?*

One woman, after writing about her family, exclaimed, "I didn't realize it was going to be so hard! All this anger started bubbling up in me." Who was the anger for? How did it feel? Where was it in your body (always good questions to write about)? The woman continued, "It started right down in my gut, but as it surged upward, it changed into power. I felt there was power coming from inside me."

And when asked what conclusion her writing would lead her to, she replied, "I don't want my father to keep letting me down! I'm finally going to accept that he isn't the person I've been trying to make him be. I've just gotten the message that he doesn't exist only to serve my needs. I guess I was pretty self-centered, not to realize that before now. I'm excited about accepting myself and my father exactly as we are. I can foresee a whole new relationship between us, based on truth instead of fantasy."

HOW CAN I BE POWERFUL WITHOUT BEING OVERPOWERING?

The problem many people have with power is that they confuse power of the spirit with power of the ego. At the level of the ego, we battle to control, dominate, and manipulate based on our fear. At the level of spirit, we simply exist and express ourselves.

Expressing your *spirit* powerfully will usually energize those around you. On the other hand, expressing your *ego* powerfully may make others feel unsafe around you. (And, of course, someone else who is accustomed to expressing his or her ego powerfully in relationship to you may resist your decision to express your spirit. It may be perceived as threatening to the control he or she held over you. The balance of your relationship may have to shift.)

Your becoming more creative, loving, intuitive, joyful, expressive, effective, responsible, independent, sure of yourself, direct, dynamic, energetic, free, and true to who you are stands to benefit others greatly. Do you seek this at the expense of anyone else?

Ask yourself about the perceived threats attached to your power: *What is it I seek to express powerfully? Who is threatened? In what ways might I respond to their fear? Can I trust myself to use my power wisely? What will my world be like when I am expressing my power openly and honestly?*

Write your answers in your workbook.

HOW CAN I BE NURTURING WITHOUT BEING TAKEN ADVANTAGE OF?

Make sure you're not taking advantage of anyone else. Do you need to be needed? If some part of your self-worth is based on what you're giving to others, then you may be using them. Such a relationship will inevitably be exposed as one of two people taking advantage of each other.

So what is your motive in being nurturing? What do you expect to receive in return? If the other person were to reject you, would it make any difference in your willingness to offer nurturing? If so, then your "nurturing" may not be nurturing at all, but a pact to get what you need, in disguise.

Give nurturing out of your best self, without conditions or anticipation of returns. Do not do what you are not willing to do freely.

Nurturing is a two-way street in healthy relationships. Develop an awareness of the balance of give-and-take in your relationships. A relationship that feels draining is one to take a second look at: What about it induces you to give more than you want to give? What are you "buying," at such an expensive price? Do you choose to maintain that state of affairs? What will you do?

Open up your workbook to make a list of people who take advantage of you, or people you suspect may start taking advantage of you. Then write a second list of people you take advantage of. Write about what you need and have tried mistakenly to get from these relationships. Write about how your needs can be met without taking advantage of others. Write how to bring balance and joy into your relationships. Summarize your learning by writing in your Dream Journal.

AM I DECEIVING MYSELF?

Ask yourself: *If I were deceiving myself, what lies would I tell myself? What is the truth I'd want to avoid knowing? What is the image of myself I want to preserve? What would I have to admit?* Write the answers in your workbook. Take some time in your Dream Journal and write a catchy affirmation to remind yourself of this learning.

Write a character study of yourself, as if an empathetic friend who truly understands you did it. Then write at the top of a clean page, "What do I *really* want, and how can I best achieve it?" Write freely any thoughts that come to mind, including objections and *"yes, buts."* After each objection, return to the question of "What do I really want?" Summarize by writing in *The Live Your Dream Workbook.*

WHAT ABOUT THE SIDE OF MYSELF I JUST CAN'T STAND?

Draw a picture in your workbook of yourself, divided down the middle into "the light side" and "the dark side." Write on each side various traits that characterize that side. Then remove each characteristic from the dark side by drawing other people—people in your life you "can't stand"— to project those characteristics onto. (Note that someone who displays a trait you "can't stand" usually represents some aspect of *yourself* that you have been unwilling to acknowledge.)

You may want to take your original drawing and cut it in half. (Note that you now have half a person, surrounded by other people you "can't stand.")

Pretend that you are a concerned coach and that your task is to interview each of these other "intolerable" people. Sympathetically question them until you understand what purpose their undesirable characteristics serve. Write the questions in your workbook that you would ask, as well as the answers they give. What reasons do you perceive for their adopting such undesirable characteristics? Write out your recommendations for helping them to be more effective and to love themselves more.

Finally, close your eyes and reclaim each of your "dark side" characteristics. See yourself joining with each of the other "undesirable" persons you have interviewed and thanking each for the new understanding he or she has given you. See yourself as unified with all these people and with all of the elements within yourself. Open your eyes and draw a new picture.

Reread what you wrote and set up a dream-partner session to discuss.

I'M LIVING MY DREAM, BUT I CAN'T PAY MY BILLS

How can I make enough money to support myself, doing just what I love to do? This is a question often asked by people who are beginning to confront the realities of living their dream. Sit down with your Dream Journal and visualize yourself living your dream to the hilt. Ask yourself: *What is my predominant need for self-expression? How do I most love to express myself? What part do other people play in the dream? How do others benefit from my living my dream? What are the benefits they would be happy to pay me for?* Record your answers in your workbook and jot down any other questions, in your journal, that occur to you to be answered as you pursue your dream and take the necessary dream steps along the way.

Then ask: *Where have I stopped short of what it takes? What more would I have to do to be completely successful? Where am I, on a time line of living my dream from beginning to end? What have I accomplished so far, and what remains that I'm going to have to do?* Plot these events on a scale that pictures the time line of your dream.

Is there any part of your dream that is consistent with being irresponsible about paying your bills? Of course not! It would be counterproductive and self-defeating. So what is your transition plan for moving toward living your dream *and* paying your bills—in other words, remaining responsible throughout this shift? Create a time line in your workbook and refer back to it often. Use your time line to plan out each day, month, and year to remain on track and to keep your focus.

How Do I Get Out of This Slump?

First ask yourself: *Do I* want *to get out of this slump? What's stopping me?* Write a dialogue in your Dream Journal between two characters: the person who *loves* (or at least has some attachments to) the slump you're in and the person who is chomping at the bit to get going. What is the first person avoiding? What makes the second person give in to that argument? Let the two characters each debate their positions until a mediator enters, promising them that a dream step can be realized if they can arrive at some resolution of their differences that satisfies the needs of both.

To consolidate your learning, make up a slogan or design a saying for a fortune cookie that summarizes your newfound wisdom. Write it down in your workbook and Dream Journal.

How Can I Get Someone to Change?

Write a list titled "The behaviors of _____ (the person's name) _____ that cause problems for me." Then next to each behavior, write a list of specific changes you'd like the person in question to make. Write about how your life might be different if the person changed. How would you be affected by these changes? How would *you* be different? How do *you* want to be?

Explore your options, deciding to be the way *you* want to be, *whether or not* the other person changes. Why are you using him or her as your excuse, anyway? Why not drive separately, if being on time is important to you and the other person is always late? Go ahead and take the workshop that person isn't interested in—by yourself. Start your diet now; don't wait until the other person changes his or her style of eating and cooking. Make the decision that *you* choose to put low-calorie foods into your mouth.

Ask yourself: *Would* I *want to be in a relationship with* me*? Why?* Write a list of changes you will make in yourself in *The Live Your Dream Workbook*.

Consider discussing your concerns with the other person. What changes would he or she like *you* to make? What kind of agreement might be negotiated? Sit down together as each of you writes, "The changes _____ (the other person) _____ can expect me to be making are _____." Post your writing where it will remind you to keep your agreement. Schedule a follow-up meeting in one week to discuss any changes either person wants to make in their agreement and to evaluate your learning so far.

Sylvia was a woman I coached whose perpetual refrain concerned her mother's interference in her life. Sylvia was 50 years old. "If she would only leave me alone," Sylvia complained. "If only I could make my own decisions without having to take my mother into consideration."

When Sylvia came to understand that her decisions had nothing to do with her mother, she began to shift her focus to deciding what *she* wanted to do with her life. Soon she no longer needed to complain; she was too busy. Within a year, Sylvia's mother started a new business of her own, saying, "I guess I'll just have to start living my dream, too!" Sylvia was astounded that the changes she made in herself had "magically" precipitated the changes she had started out wanting her *mother* to make.

WILL I HAVE TO LEAVE MY PRESENT RELATIONSHIP?

Read and then write to answer the following questions:

✦ Does my current relationship support me in living my dream?

✦ What's working in my relationship?

✦ What's not working in my relationship?

✦ Is my partner aware of my needs and desires?

✦ Are my needs and desires important in our relationship?

✦ What do I need in this relationship?

✦ What is the purpose of our relationship?

✦ What holds me in this relationship?

✦ Am I being completely honest with myself and with my partner? If not, what is it that it's time to communicate? What do I want my partner to know?

✦ If I stay in this relationship, what changes will need to occur in order for me to realize my dream?

✦ What have I learned from this exercise so far? Summarize in *The Live Your Dream Workbook*.

Each time you move to a new level of living your dream or expanding your dream, new demands will be made on all your relationships. You will either communicate, tell the truth, make needed adjustments, and grow, or your relationships will be at risk of becoming outdated and dysfunctional.

Do these questions sound selfish and self-centered? Ah! That's a wonderful question, because on the surface it may seem selfish to keep focusing on what *you* want. But at a deeper level, these questions form the foundation for a solidly grounded relationship, in which you don't cheat the person you're with because you're knowing and being yourself. With your own wants and needs satisfied, your energy is freed to share and express yourself with others. The emphasis shifts from being *self-centered* to being *self-actualized.* In such a relationship, each person says to the other,

"Oh, I see—you want to do that! What can I do to make it a win for both of us, as I do what I'll be doing to realize and live my dream, too?"

Any relationship can last, I believe, if both persons maintain the desire and the commitment to keep it alive and growing. My relationship with my husband is constantly evolving from one day to the next. It thrives on the continual focus on results and what each of us wants. "What can I do to support you in getting what you want?" is a question we ask each other almost daily. And, of course, shared dreams are incredibly important in a relationship, too.

So use the questions in this section repeatedly, whenever it's time to rethink the parameters of all your relationships. And keep your focus firmly set on results and how to bring them about. Become an *actualized dreamer.*

WHEN YOU COULD USE SOME PRAISE

Write a letter to yourself! Be sure to do this whenever you've had a wonderful experience or a magnificent success. Give yourself lavish compliments, and acknowledge your successes. Re-create the glowing feeling you have and emphasize your effective role in bringing it about. Congratulate yourself for choosing to live your dream fully, and give yourself lots of love. Seal your letter in an envelope, and write on the outside the date or occasion on which you will open and read it, such as:

FOR (*your name*). OPEN ON A DAY WHEN YOU COULD USE SOME PRAISE.

IF YOUR DREAM GROWS FAINT

Reading my Dream Statement over whenever my dream begins to feel faded brings back the inspiration and rejuvenating energy I felt when I originally wrote about it. As soon as I review the work I've scheduled for my three-month, six-month, and one-year plans, I sit up and realize, "I'd better get busy!"

If your dream is growing faint, go back and read the inspiring sections you have written in your Dream Journal and *The Live Your Dream Workbook* about your dream. Then ask yourself: *Is it time to update my Dream Statement or my Dream Plans?*

Write down every demonstration that shows you are living your dream. Share your successes with others. Consciously strengthen your commitment to living your dream by repeatedly writing, "I know I have the desire to live my dream because _____ ," and completing it with many different answers. Assign yourself to produce one measurable result each day that is part of bringing your dream into reality.

Then, to serve as a rejuvenating reminder, choose a song that captures the excitement of your dream. Get a recording of it and play it often.

How Long Do I Have to Keep Working on My Dream?

This is a question I am often asked. I always laugh and reply, "As long as you want to keep bringing all your dreams into reality." I encourage people to do whatever works best to keep their dreams alive: take classes, read books, form a support group, hire an expert, start a Dream Circle, hire a Dream Coach. To reassess your progress and reaffirm your commitment to living your dream, write about the following:

+ What are the signs that I'm experiencing my dream?

+ What accomplishments have I achieved in the past six months?

+ Which assignments did I avoid?

+ What changes am I avoiding making?

+ What's the *big* step I haven't taken yet?

+ What have I done in the past to revitalize myself?

Your Dream Come True

And now, here's one final writing exercise that is extremely valuable for achieving your dream. Also, it can serve as a revitalizer when you read it over months or years from now.

Storytellers, wizards, magicians, giants, fairy godmothers, medicine men, and so on have very likely been a part of your life and your development. Therefore, my invitation to add a little creative writing to your dreamwork will not surprise you.

Write your story! Write the story that pictures you living the dream you have claimed. Take from 30 minutes to an hour and write in your Dream Journal. Include a descriptive setting that portrays you, your feelings, your environment, and other involved characters. Allow your words to draw the pictures for you. Incorporate your values, motivators, wishes, hopes, and dreams into your plot, and write a story climax that shows how all the dream work you've done has paid off in wonderful ways. Read your dream novel to your dream partner and to other significant people in your life whom you can count on to support you in living your dream.

Here are some examples from dreamers just like you:

Lissa's Dream Novel

Awakening early, without an alarm clock, I feel refreshed, peaceful, and confident as I look forward to the day. My imagination is ignited for my present writing project. After feeding the pets, I head for the computer, excited to have the time, energy, and focus to get right to it.

Several of my works have already been published, earning both critical and financial rewards. They have found a large appreciative audience, entertained and enlightened by what I have to say and how I say it.

My spiritual life is richer than ever because I have increased my ability to hear and follow divine guidance. I have learned to surrender what no longer serves me and to trust that what I need is provided. No matter what is going on in my life I feel capable of handling it, knowing the appropriate action and when to take it.

I continue to grow in wisdom and peace through reading, journaling, theater, lectures, traveling, and relationships with others. In addition to family, my support network includes groups and individuals also living their dreams, reaching to fulfill their soul's purpose.

Continually inspired by the magic and mystery in everyday life, I urge others to find it as well. My writing is balanced with the highest use of my skills as a counselor, assisting individuals and groups to the best use of themselves. This evening I will be facilitating a group where my skills as storyteller and counselor will be balanced for the highest good of all concerned.

Writing can take center stage in my life now because I live in a financial comfort zone. I am debt-free and have what I need to support me. With energy drains no longer blocking the flow of light, creative inspiration shines. I also contribute generously to individuals and organizations that are making a difference on the planet.

My home is my sanctuary and sacred space, beautiful to me inside and out. That which was broken is repaired. That which I no longer need has been released. Outside I have my own secret garden, a place that nurtures me and connects me to spirit whenever I step into it.

Now physically healthy, I have created for myself a "fun-for-me exercise plan." Both my breathing and body flexibility are great, giving me the energy and stamina needed to handle "real world" matters efficiently.

Peace in the world is growing, as more and more people understand that we are one human family with more similarities than differences. By contributing to all the people in my life with empathy, compassion, humor, and a loving heart, I serve the vision of world peace and union.

I am living my life as the minister of magical merriment, a channel for the light, entertaining, enlightening, and empowering all those who cross my path.

Lianne's Dream Novel

Never before had she felt such peace, such inner calm. Never before had she held her own strength so completely. Never before had she felt so complete. Pleasing everyone was no longer an issue in her life. Pleasing herself was fulfilling her in every way. She was in a strong position. She could choose—anything she wanted, and direction to go in, any place to travel. The work she was doing was fullfilling her in every way, and was bringing in a good living. She was independent. She could choose....

She walked from the beautiful, earthy house of her dreams into the magnificent garden and breathed in the sweet, heavy evening air. She looked around her, at the house—this house of her dreams, with its Garden of Eden, filled with lush green grass, robust oak and fruit trees, bushes, and creepers. It was wild and jungle like with lots of bright, exotic flowers of all colors, and filled with the loud chirping of euphoric birds, drunk with abundance.

In the evenings after sunset, she would sit out on the veranda, looking at the night-blue lake beyond the garden, and hear grasshoppers finding their soul mates under the powerful magic of the bright, iridescent moon. Stillness, quiet, close to nature, yet not far away from the people she loved and near enough to the excitement and bustle of the city to aid with the conveniences of the life she led. Her big, cream-colored Labrador came bounding up and she knew the laughter and shrieks of her three children were not far behind. She patted the dog's soft, silky head and closed her eyes, remembering the past, with a grateful prayer of thanks on her lips for the present. What a gift it was to be living this life of her dreams, with light in her soul, unencumbered. What a gift to have been able to channel her healing energy and build her dream of helping others empower themselves. That is what she had come here to do: to help others see light in their lives and achieve their life's purpose. What a gift she was no longer stuck in the misery of pain and struggling.

Her thoughts rolled back five years, to when it all began, to when she, with the invaluable support of five very close friends, began a process of self-empowerment and release, in order to let go of old and painful patterns. She remembered clearly the day she had said to her son, "Oran, this for me, is a dream come true. I always knew, deep down inside, that becoming thin and healthy did not have to mean pain, deprivation, and suffering." She always knew that if she could only find the right keys to unlock the blocked chambers of her heart, she could fulfill her dream of trusting her body to do the right thing for itself. That deprivation had no part here, not for her body and not for her soul. It was all a matter of choice. And if she helped herself make the right choices, she could trust her body to heal itself and be healthy. The 35kg she lost, the chains that bound her virtually all her life, had gone effortlessly, with joy and trust, and had become a metaphor for the way she would approach the rest of her life, forever.

Beverly's Dream Novel

Never had life been more perfect. Each segment of Bev's busy yet carefree schedule ran without a hitch. The dream was now a reality for Beverly, and she savored every moment.

Spiritually alive, she awakened each morning to the sound of the waves rushing to the shore outside her beachfront home and began the day with the meditations she had grown to cherish, prefaced with some inspirational reading. Peaceful moments alone with the munificent Universe were the bulwark of a full, rich day of work and play. Beverly participated in a blend of yoga and walks along the shore to reinforce her connection to the Divine. Reading and following her own inner truth had rounded out the path of spirituality so vital to her balance. It was a bonus, she considered, that she was able to share her love of truth with the rest of her family.

Family—the foundation of her reason for joy. Her daughter Kate was in her final year of law school, with an offer already in hand for an apprenticeship in a fine Washington, D.C. law firm. Kelly was enjoying her sophomore year at the small local college and had recently been elected homecoming queen. Kirk, Beverly's son, would soon be graduated from high school with honors and had already been accepted to both Harvard and Stanford. And although John had joined the family only recently (a "dad" to the children and loving husband to Beverly), his warmth and generous love brightened every day.

Their home was a demonstration of the beauty and serenity felt by each member. An expanse of glass in the living room reflected the sparkle of the California coast. The muted colors of nature decorated the exquisite interior of the sizable home.

Beverly's attention to her physical well-being was evident in her firm, trim body. Daily exercise was the norm. Regular tennis was interspersed with ongoing yoga. Beverly's organized shopping plan had paid off with a well-coordinated closet—the latest fashions accented by tasteful jewels facilitated her desire to always look her best. The holidays would be filled with family entertaining and gatherings at the homes of their many friends. All the kids would be home, filling the house with their own friends and their laughter. Christmas week would culminate with a midnight champagne buffet for a host of friends and family. Even now, the decoration process had begun. Fine ornaments and strands of white twinkling lights and pearls rounded out the stately tree, reminiscent of a romantic, Victorian era.

Beverly's mental agility and productivity had been challenged in her job where she was the top producer in a brokerage house. An abundance of money had long since ceased to be her motivation, and she now produced beyond her wildest dreams for the sheer joy of it. Well-earned respect and accolades were the fruits of her commitment and dedication to her dream. And the community work now funded by her firm—because of her diligent persistence—served hundreds of people every week.

Tomorrow was to be such a special day for Beverly and her two closest friends. As a surprise for one friend's birthday, Beverly had arranged for a private jet to fly the trio to San Francisco for a day of shopping, lunch and a new hit play. Champagne, love, and laughter would be their watchwords. The expectation of their merriment brought a smile to her face.

Lynn's Dream Novel

A quiver of exhilaration surged through her, as the rapturous theme of Dvorak's *New World* Symphony rose and enveloped Lynn in its mystical beauty, luring her attention away from the work on her desk, and laying full claim to her imagination. Willingly surrendering to its inspiration, she leaned back in her easy chair and closed her eyes to receive the gift of the music. The beauty of the surrounding room enveloped her, lending an aura of its own to the magic of the moment.

A procession of happy thoughts paraded past her consciousness. The latest manuscript—a brilliant, delightfully humorous, inspirational work—was expertly developed and complete; she would deliver it with pride and confidence the following day, to a meeting with her publisher halfway around the world.

The traveling was always a special part of this work, meeting such engaging and bright people and staying in interesting new places for a few days, especially when she was able to bring her son Brendan along. Such an amazing child, that delightful boy, curious and eager to learn about everything, so intelligent and so much fun. And other times when her new beau would accompany her: the delight of going exploring together, of discovering beauty beyond the ordinary, insights into each other from a new perspective, the mutual support given and received in the intimate way that is possible when two people communicate openly and fully out of love.

And the traveling was but a small part of Lynn's ever-enriching life. Probably more than anything else, she loved the opportunity of bringing love into the lives of the many people whose appreciation for her work had brought her so many rewards. She glanced up fondly at the bookshelf of best-selling books she had written. It was a satisfying contribution to make to the world. She could only feel thankful for the guidance she'd received in realizing her utmost potential. The endowments and gifts she sent to organizations doing wonderful work represented being able to give back a small part of what she had received.

As the final strains of the symphony died down, Lynn roused herself from her reflections. A brief stroll through her flower garden, before she would eagerly resume writing. The next project was rapidly taking shape.

It is with joy and excitement that I include this last dream novel. It is also an excellent example of one of my dreams coming true. Since the very beginning workshop I knew that someday I wanted others to take the step-by-step program I had designed and to train to teach/facilitate *Live Your Dream* all over the world! I had the confidence that my years of research and own personal learning created a curriculum that would make living true to one's self and following one's dream a popular concept!

Sherry Laness is a "Live Your Dream"certified facilitator who will definitely assist and empower me and others through her extraordinary commitment to her dreams!

It's five in the morning. The first birds are chirping. A rooster crows. Sherry wakes up. Her first thoughts are, *Wow! What a wonderful day this is and what fun I'm going to have today!* Sherry says a Hebrew prayer: "I give thanks before you, living and existing King/Queen, for returning my soul to me. Great is Your belief in me." With a stretch, Sherry jumps out of bed.

Quickly dressing and lacing her walking shoes, Sherry glances at her weekly schedule. She notices what is planned for the day, the week, and the month ahead and is filled with pleasure and gratitude for a life that is so fulfilling. This morning, there is the opening of a "Live Your Dream" workshop in Hebrew, with a group of 24 men and women who are training to be "Live Your Dream" workshop facilitators. Tonight, is the "If I Had Three Wishes, The Only One Would Be!" workshop with 18 participants. Tonight's meeting is the third one and the group is so inspired and inspiring! Tomorrow she is addressing a combined session of the Education and the Defense Ministry, who are interested in her proposal of having the "Live Your

Dream" team offer "Live Your Dream" workshops to soldiers finishing their service, as a way of entering civilian life with a purpose and a dream.

Next week begins a three-day retreat with the other "Live Your Dream" facilitators in the region. It is the first such event of it's kind. Attending will be facilitators from Israel, Jordan, Palestine, Egypt, England, France, Holland, Germany, Greece, Switzerland, Hungary, Italy, Turkey, Kuwait, Bahrain, Iran, and Iraq. Some have trained with Joyce Chapman, and some Sherry has trained. They will be meeting in a wonderful village that is known for its health food and healthy air. And there, they will dream endlessly together! Joyce Chapman is giving the opening address and will be attending the conference as our coach and mentor. Sherry is co-chairing the event. It has been a most exciting time, preparing for this regional conference. She is looking forward to meeting Joyce at the airport and accompanying her to her hotel. They will have dinner together and speak about the plans for the conference. It is always a joy and an inspiration when Joyce comes to Israel!

Sherry steps out of her beautiful, large, country home as the night turns to day and she pats her cats and smiles. It is all as she had imagined and planned it. There are the fruit trees with lemons, oranges, mangoes, pomegranates, and loquats. There is her vegetable garden with tomatoes, cucumbers, lettuce, parsley, dill, cabbages, cauliflower, zucchini, eggplant, peppers, and a variety of spices. Her gardening time is a time of renewing her strength and power and she loves it, although she also has the help of a professional organic gardener who comes once a month to help with any questions that arise. Sherry sniffs the clear morning air and is filled with pleasure.

And now, she's off for her power walk. Sherry loves these walks. This is her time to commune with nature, with her Creator, with her inner voice, with her dreams, and a time to let the vision of the day and days-ahead sweep through her. She calls it her Power-Meditation Walk.

After her shower and healthy breakfast, Sherry goes to her office. It is in a separate part of house and is entered through an outside door. No one disturbs her there. It is her workplace and *hers alone.* The large glass doors overlook her garden. There she works on materials for her workshops, lectures, and overseas programs. There she takes her phone calls from workshop participants and people who she is training. There she meditates and listens to music while her spirit renews itself and soars. It is her sanctuary. She looks at her latest Dream Board, and remembers who she is and who she wants to be.

Sherry opens the adjoining door to her fabulous workshop room. *This is just what I have always wanted,* she thinks to herself.

The room is bright, clean, and shining with wonderful posters, paintings, sayings, plants, flowers, and various textures of fabrics on the furniture. It is a perfect place for the wonderful workshops she gives. It has already been set up for the next workshop by Sherry's fabulous assistant. Her assistant not only has a wonderful sense of style, but also types and does most of the publicity work for Sherry. What a treasure she is!

Sherry once again glances at her schedule, this time for the coming months. She remembers that she is now a master facilitator, a coach, and a trainer of others. She blesses the day that she found the *Live Your Dream* book and began her journey to her dream.

And speaking of journeys, Sherry notices that soon she will be going on one of her dream trips. This time, it is to China. As with all of her dream trips, Edo, her loving husband, is her adventurous companion. They have so much fun together, both on trips and at home. They have a rich life of concerts, plays, friends, parties, and celebrations with family. It is a joy to have such a wonderful partner who supports her dream and also lives his life fully.

Sherry's children are all grown and self-reliant and living their dreams. It is so inspiring to see the different roads they have chosen and to be updated regularly at family gatherings and celebrations as well as by phone. And the grandchildren are healthy and growing to be the extraordinary human beings, as Sherry hopes every person in the world will grow up to be. Her children and their spouses love and respect her and often visit, and they know how busy she is, so they always call first.

Sherry also knows that she will spend a week with her mother and sister next month. It is so important to her to enjoy her family and be a part of their lives even though they live on different continents. And she thinks about how they have succeeded in seeing each other at least twice a year for the last several years. And her weekly calls to her mother and sister are warm and loving and inspiring, as they are living their dreams as well.

Sherry relaxes into her comfortable chair and sits down to journal. Her journal, which at first seemed so intimidating, has become her closest friend and confidant. It is there that she writes her dream-life into reality: "It is such a wonderful day to live my dream!"

Your own story may he longer or shorter than these examples. You can add to it as your vision and your dreams grow. Be sure to describe all the various aspects of the dream life you envision: career, self-expression, relationship, finances, home, family, recreation, and so on.

Set aside time for reading and updating your story on New Year's Day every year.

Five-year-old Cathy, who had come into the shoe store knowing exactly what kind of shoes she wanted, asked the salesperson, "Do you know *everything* about shoes?" The reply was, "Well, sort of." Cathy asked incredulously, "Then *why* are you selling them?" The salesperson stepped back and allowed herself to hear an important message: If you are living your life by "sort ofs," what *sort of* result can you expect?

Will you be the main character in your own life? Will your life be a daring adventure or nothing?

This is your life! Now that you have finished this book, go right back and start again. Experience shows that the person who grows is the one who starts the process all over again as soon as they have reached the goal of one dream.

See it!

Claim it!

Create it!

Celebrate it!

Suggested Reading List for Enjoyment and Expansion

The following bibliography is the original list I complied in 1990. I now recommend that you begin to add to this list, visit Web sites, and make reading, learning, and researching part of your journey. I also advise you to read each of my books:

✦ *Live Your Dream: Discover and Achieve Your Life Purpose: A Step-By-Step Program*

✦ *The Live Your Dream Workbook: Discover & Live the Life of Your Dreams*

✦ *Journaling For Joy: Writing Your Way to Personal Growth and Freedom*

✦ *Journaling For Joy: Writing Your Way to Personal Growth and Freedom (workbook)*

✦ *If I Had Three Wishes, the Only One Would Be: Your Personalized Plan for Discovering Your Life Goals, Igniting Your Spirit Power, and Making Your Dreams Come True*

✦ *If I Had Three Wishes, the Only One Would Be :Your Personalized Plan for Discovering Your Life Goals, Igniting Your Spirit Power, and Making Your Dreams Come Alive (workbook)*

Allen, James. As *a Man Thinketh*. Sun Publishers, 1983.

Andrews, Lynn V. *Jaguar Woman*. Harper & Row, 1986.

Assagioli, Roberto. *Act of Will*. Penguin, 1974.

——. *Psychosynthesis*. Penguin, 1971.

Bach, Richard. *Illusions: The Adventures of a Reluctant Messiah*. Delacorte, 1977.

Baer, Jean. *How to Be an Assertive (Not Aggressive) Woman in Life, Love, and on the Job: A Total Guide to Self-Assertiveness.* New American Library, Signet Books, 1976.

Beattie, Melody. *Codependent No More: How to Stop Controlling Others and Start Caring for Yourself.* Hazelden, 1988.

Blanchard, Kenneth, and Spencer Johnson. *The One Minute Manager.* Berkley, 1987.

Bloomfield, Harold and Leonard Felder. *Making Peace with Your Parents.* Random, 1983.

Bowers, Barbara. *What Color Is Your Aura? Personality Spectrums for Understanding and Growth.* Pocket Books, 1989.

Branden, Nathaniel. *How to Raise Your Self-Esteem.* Bantam, 1987.

Brenner, Paul. Health Is a Question of Balance. DeVorss, 1980.

Briggs, Dorothy Corkille. Celebrate Your Self. Doubleday, 1977.

Buzan, Tony. *Use Both Sides of Your Brain.* E. P. Dutton, 1983.

Capacchione, Lucia. *The Creative Journal: The* Art *of Finding Yourself.* By arrangement with Ohio University Press. Newcastle Publishing Co., 1989.

Cole-Whittaker, Terry. *What You Think of Me Is None of My Business.* Oak Tree Publications, 1982.

Dass, Ram. *Journey of Awakening: A Meditator's Guidebook.* Bantam, 1982.

Davis, et al. *Relaxation and Stress Reduction.* New Harbinger, 1982.

Dychtwald, Ken. *Bodymind.* J. P. Tarcher, 1986.

Dyer, Wayne W. *Choosing Your Own Greatness.* Nightingale-Conant, 1989.

———. *Your Erroneous Zones.* Avon, 1977.

Ferguson, Marilyn. *The Aquarian Conspiracy: Personal and Social Transformation in the 1980s.* J.P. Tarcher, 1987.

Fields, Rick, Taylor, Weyler, and Ingrasci. *Chop Wood, Carry Water: A Guide to Finding Spiritual Fulfillment in Everyday Life.* J. P. Tarcher, 1984.

Foster, Steven, and Meredith Little. *The Book of the Vision Quest: Personal Transformation in the Wilderness.* Prentice-Hall, 1988.

Foundation for Inner Peace. A *Course in Miracles.* Foundation for Inner Peace, 1985.

Fox, Emmet. *The Mental Equivalent.* Unity School of Christianity, 1984.

Fromm, Erich. *The Art of Loving.* Harper & Row, 1974.

Gawain, Shakti. *Creative Visualization.* New World Publishers, 1978.

Gillies, Jerry. *Moneylove.* Warner Books, 1979.

Gilman, Dorothy. *A New Kind of Country.* Double Day & Company, Inc., 1978.

Goldberg, Natalie. *Writing Down the Bones: Freeing the Writer Within.* Shamhhala Publications, 1986.

Haas, Robert. *Eat to Win: The Sports Nutrition Bible.* New American Library, 1985.

Hanley, John. *Lifespring: Getting Yourself from Where You Are to Where You Want to Be.* Simon & Schuster, 1989.

Hesse, Hermann. *Siddhartha.* Bantam, 1982.

Hoffman, Bob. *No One Is to Blame: Getting a Loving Divorce from Mom and Dad.* Science & Behavior, 1979.

Holmes, Ernest. *The Science of Mind.* Dodd, Mead & Co., 1938.

Houston, Jean. *The Possible Human: A Course in Extending Your Physical, Mental, and Creative Abilities.* J. P. Tarcher, 1982.

Iluang, Chung-Liang Al. *Quantum Soup: A Philosophical Entertainment.* Dutton, 1983.

Jampoisky, Gerald G. *Love Is Letting Go of Fear.* Bantam, 1982.

Jeffers, Susan. *Feel the Fear and Do It Anyway.* Harcourt Brace Jovanovich, 1987.

——. *Opening Our Hearts to Men.* Fawcett, 1989.

Johnson, Spencer. *One Minute for Myself: How to Manage Your Most Valuable Asset.* Avon, 1987.

Josefowitz, Natasha. *Is This Where I Was Going?* Warner, 1983.

——. *Paths to Power: A Woman's Guide from First Job to Top Executive.* Addison-Wesley, 1980.

Josefowitz, Natasha and Herman Gadon. *Fitting In: How to Get a Good Start in Your New Job.* Addison-Wesley, 1988.

Joy, W. Brugh. *Joy's Way.* J. P. Tarcher, 1979.

Keyes, Ken, Jr. *The Hundredth Monkey.* Vision Books, 1982.

Klauser, Henriette A. *Writing on Both Sides of the Brain: Breakthrough Techniques for People Who Write.* Harper & Row, 1986.

Kubler-Ross, Elisabeth. *On Death and Dying.* Macmillan, 1970.

Lama Foundation Staff. *Be Here Now.* Crown, 1971.

Lenz, Marjorie and Marjorie Hansen Shaevitz. *So You Want to Go Back to School.* McGraw, 1977.

Lerner, Harriet Goldhor. *The Dance of Anger: A Woman's Guide to Changing the Patterns of Intimate Relationships.* Harper & Row, 1985.

MacLaine, Shirley. *Out on a Limb.* Bantam, 1983.

Maltz, Maxwell. *Psycho-Cybernetics.* Pocket Books, Inc., 1983.

Mandino, Og. *The Greatest Miracle in the World.* Bantam, 1983.

Millman, Dan. *Way of the Peaceful Warrior: A Book That Changes Lives.* H.J. Kramer, 1984.

Noble, Vicki. *Motherpeace: A Way to the Goddess Through Myth, Art and Tarot.* Harper & Row, 1982.

Norwood, Robin. *Women Who Love Too Much: When You Keep Wishing and Hoping He'll Change.* J.P. Archer, 1985.

Peck, M. Scott. *The Road Less Traveled.* Touchstone Books, Simon & Schuster, 1980.

Pelletier, Kenneth R. *Mind As Healer, Mind As Slayer: A Holistic Approach to Preventing Stress Disorders.* Peter Smith, 1984.

Phelps, Stanlee and Nancy Austin. *The Assertive Woman.* Impact, 1975.

Ponder, Catherine. *The Dynamic Laws of Prosperity.* DeVorss, 1985.

Prather, Hugh. *A Book of Games: A Course in Spiritual Play.* Doubleday, 1981.

Prather, Hugh, and Gayle Prather. *A Book for Couples.* Doubleday, 1988.

Price, John Randolph. *The Superbeings.* Fawcett, 1987.

Ray, Sondra. *I Deserve Love.* Celestial Arts, 1987.

——. *Loving Relationships.* Celestial Arts, 1980.

Shaevitz, Marjorie Hansen. *The Superwoman Syndrome.* Warner, 1985.

Shaevitz, Morton H. and Marjorie Hansen Shaevitz. *Making It Together: As a Career Couple.* Houghton Mifflin, 1980.

Shinn, Florence Scovel. *Your Word Is Your Wand.* DeVorss, 1978.

Siegel, Bernard S. *Love, Medicine and Miracles.* Harper & Row, 1986.

Silva, Jose and Philip Miele. *The Silva Mind Control Method.* Pocket Books, 1978.

Simonton, Carl, et al. *Getting Well Again.* Bantam, 1982.

Stoddard, Alexandra. *Living a Beautiful Life: Five Hundred Ways to Add Elegance, Order, Beauty and Joy to Every Day of Your Life.* Avon, 1988.

Szekely, Edmond B. *Creative Work: Karma Yoga.* IBS International, 1973.

Teilhard de Chardin, Pierre. *Phenomenon of Man.* Harper & Row, 1965.

Thoreau, Henry David. *The Journal of Henry D. Thoreau.* Princeton University Press, 1984.

Toben, Bob and Fred A. Wolf. *Space-Time and Beyond (Physics Explains the Unexplainable).* Dutton, 1982.

Tver, David F. and Howard F. Hunt. *Encyclopedic Dictionary of Sports Medicine (Advanced Industrial Technology Series).* Routledge Chapman & Hall, 1986.

Watts, Alan W. *This Is It.* Random, 1972.

Woititz, Janet G. *Adult Children of Alcoholics.* Health Communications, 1983.

Wonder, Jacquelyn and Priscilla Donovan. Whole-Brain Thinking: Working from Both Sides of the Brain to Achieve Peak Job Performance. Ballantine, 1985.

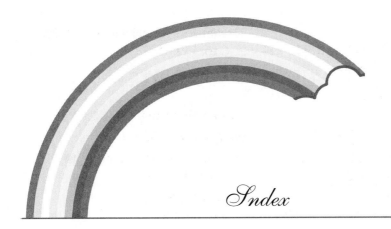

Index

About the Author

*J*oyce Chapman, M.A., is a dream coach dedicated to living true to herself, her dreams and inspiring others to do the same. She offers a home-study program for individuals who want the guidance of an expert as their dreams become more exciting and challenging. For those individuals who want to use the step-by-step program presented in this book and become part of an international dream team to facilitate and coach, she offers a training and certification program.

In addition *to Live Your Dream: Discover and Achieve Your Life Purpose*, Joyce is the author of *The Live Your Dream Workbook: Discover and Live The Life of Your Dream, Journaling For Joy: Writing Your Way to Personal Growth and Freedom; The Workbook ~ Journaling For Joy: Writing Your Way to Personal Growth and Freedom; If I Had Three Wishes the Only One Would Be...: Your Personalized Plan for Discovering Your Life Goals, Igniting Your Spirit Power, and Making Your Dreams Come Alive;* and *The Workbook ~ If I Had Three Wishes the Only One Would Be...:Your Personalized Plan for Discovering Your Life Goals, Igniting Your Spirit Power, and Making Your Dreams Come Alive.*

Joyce Chapman's professional background includes 18 years as a teacher and teacher trainer in the California public school system and two years as founder/director of an innovative private school. She has a master's degree in counseling psychology. Joyce has been combining and utilizing her life and educational experiences for more than 40 years to serve at the highest level she is capable of achieving. She is well known as a pioneer in the fields of personal and professional coaching. Her intention is to create and design programs that will enrich and empower the lives of her readers, clients, and workshop participants until the end of her life.

She is also extremely proud to share her life wishes, hopes, and dreams as a wife, a mother of four grown children, a grandmother of 11 grandchildren, and a friend who treasures friendship.

For more information, you may e-mail Joyce Chapman at *dreams@joycechapman.com*. Visit Joyce's Web site at *www.joycechapman.com* to join The Live Your Dream ~ Dreamcircle and subscribe to a free monthly newsletter.